Legal Culture, Sociopolitical Origins and Professional Careers of Judges in Mexico

"Focusing on subnational judges, Azul Aguiar's analysis of their legal culture reveals the slow and uneven transformation of Mexico's judiciary. Exploring judges' origins, training, recruitment, and beliefs about the law, her research makes an important methodological contribution to exploring legal culture and to comparative, ideational studies of judicial behavior."

—Rachel Sieder, *CIESAS, Mexico City*

"Azul Aguiar's exploration into the relatively unchartered territory of judicial culture in Mexico finds a colorful landscape in contrast to the grey zone that is mostly assumed. This rich sociolegal analysis is a welcome addition to the judicial and legal scholarship in Mexico and beyond."

—Julio Ríos Figueroa, *ITAM*

Azul A. Aguiar Aguilar

Legal Culture, Sociopolitical Origins and Professional Careers of Judges in Mexico

palgrave
macmillan

Azul A. Aguiar Aguilar
ITESO, Jesuit University
of Guadalajara
Tlaquepaque, Mexico

ISBN 978-3-031-52908-5   ISBN 978-3-031-52909-2 (eBook)
https://doi.org/10.1007/978-3-031-52909-2

The translation was done with the help of an artificial intelligence machine translation tool. A subsequent human revision was done primarily in terms of content.

This Palgrave Macmillan imprint is published by the registered company Springer Nature Switzerland AG
The registered company address is: Gewerbestrasse 11, 6330 Cham, Switzerland

Paper in this product is recyclable.

Ad Alberto per il suo sostegno.
Ad Aleph per la sua ispirazione.
A mis padres, por llevarme hasta aquí.

Contents

List of Figures

List of Tables

CHAPTER 1

Introduction. Unveiling the Judiciary: An Inside Perspective

Abstract This book provides an account of the sociopolitical origins and professional profiles of one of the least-studied political elites in Mexican democracy: the judges of the federal judiciary. Drawing on data collected through a survey with federal judges in Mexico, it addresses topics such as judges' family background, where they received their education, how they entered the judiciary, what types of ideas and legal conceptions they have developed, their beliefs regarding the political role of judges, as well as their opinions on rights and freedoms such as legal abortion, drug decriminalization, same-sex marriage, or the legalization of marijuana. Thus, a careful characterization of the judges' profile is presented to infer their judicial behavior based on their ideas, values, and beliefs.

Keywords Legal culture · Mexican judicial politics · Judges · Judicial career · Judiciary · Judicial elites

In Mexico, judges are often characterized as an elite group, perceived as conservative, legalistic, nepotistic, and sometimes corrupt. This perception sharply contrasts with their fundamental role in ensuring citizens' access to justice and promoting the development of a more egalitarian,

A. A. Aguiar Aguilar, *Legal Culture, Sociopolitical Origins and Professional Careers of Judges in Mexico*,
https://doi.org/10.1007/978-3-031-52909-2_1

just, and democratic society. In fact, a significant portion of the population lacks confidence in the judiciary. Judges vie with legislators and law enforcement officers for the lowest positions on the trust scale in survey studies that gauge public trust in institutions (see, for example, Latinobarómetro, 2021).

Likewise, within the academic community and among citizens who interact with the courts, the prevailing notion is that judges constitute a formalistic and insular elite, rendering decisions that appear detached from the social, political, or cultural context that surrounds them. In fact, the judicial elite, unlike others such as representatives, is even more isolated from society. Just think about how judges write their rulings and defend them in court. The average citizen, and even those with education, often find it challenging to comprehend the majority of rulings delivered by judges due to the use of an arcane technical language. Consequently, in most instances, we remain unaware of what judges decide, the methods they employ, and the rationale behind their decisions. We fail to know judges through their rulings, which is contrary to the ideal they espouse when emphasizing their independence from political authority.

Consider also how the "judicial family" operates in isolation from its public, crafting decisions within a prestigious office situated in a glass skyscraper, known to some as "Judicial City." It exists in a state of seclusion, remote and, to some extent, beyond reach for many. This city, which is usually far from urban centers, clusters district and collegiate courts: it is the heart of access to justice at the federal level, but it is difficult for the average citizen in Mexico to reach it.

Despite this, the tasks performed by the judiciary directly affect people's daily lives, but also the stability of the political regime. Judges are not like any public official. They bear the great task of discerning the validity of a right, ensuring that justice reaches those who claim and need it. They play a crucial role in resolving political disputes, which in turn helps prevent the tyranny of the majority or the destabilization of the political regime. As an example, consider the right of same-sex couples to marry and live a life free from discrimination. In our societies, marriage has traditionally been defined as "the union between a man and a woman," often accompanied by the notion of "for perpetuating the specie." For the political parties in power, altering this regulation is a highly contentious matter. Although human rights have taken center stage in the political arena, there are deeply ingrained values and ideas, such as heterosexual marriage, that hold sway within the voting community. The struggles and strategic litigation by movements advocating for sexual diversity have resulted in the judicial invalidation of legislation that, in several countries, including Mexico, defined marriage as exclusively between a man and a woman. This legal transformation has occurred because such laws contravene established principles and guarantees, including international treaties, and constitutional rights such as equality and non-discrimination. In essence, there are rights that neither the legislative nor the executive branches are adapting to the changing social and cultural context. Judges are actively involved in addressing these issues.

Consider also an electoral reform passed by law makers that erodes the principles of electoral organization and democracy by consolidating an excessive amount of power within the executive branch. In such a scenario, an independent Constitutional Court, vested with judicial review authority, would have the capacity to nullify such legislation for contravening constitutional and conventional principles designed to protect the stability and future of electoral democracy. A decision in this regard would reinforce the separation of powers and sustain the vitality of the democratic system.

It's important to note that not every judge is inclined to make expansive interpretations of individuals' rights or venture to declare a decree or law issued by elected representatives as unconstitutional. Are judges up to the task of addressing the demands of a plural, democratic, and diverse society? Do they consider themselves political actors with the ability to define public policies? Are they willing to set limits on the tyranny of the majority and defend the democratic rules? Do they have the training, professional trajectory, and ideas to expand the rights of citizens or, rather, to protect the status quo?

Despite its relevance, the existing literature on judicial politics in Mexico has not provided answers to these questions. The federal judiciary is above all an unknown institution and, until a few decades ago, was also effectively marginalized from the political system. Its organizational and constitutional structure is well documented, as it has been extensively examined by prominent legal scholars. (Cossio, 1996; Fix-Fierro, 1996; Fix-Zamudio, 1997). In fact, the judiciary in Mexico was almost exclusively a subject of study of legal scholars. However, this began to change with the process of transition to democracy. From

Mexican political science, the internal and external dynamics of the judiciary have begun to be accounted for only in the past two decades (Aguiar-Aguilar, 2022; Ansolabehere, 2007; Castagnola & López, 2016; Castillejos-Aragón, 2013; Cortez, 2020; Inclán, 2009; Ingram, 2016a; Pozas-Loyo & Ríos-Figueroa, 2010; Ríos-Figueroa, 2007; Sánchez et al., 2011). Despite being few in number, these works have been the seed of judicial politics in Mexico.

Within political science, judicial politics has analyzed the problems relating to law and politics, the institutional design of courts and judicial behavior. Its expansion begins in the 1940s in the United States and reaches Latin America with the third wave of democratizations (Aguiar-Aguilar, 2019). Judicial politics has sought to explain, on the one hand, what institutional designs favor the empowerment and activism of judges and, on the other, why judges decide in the way they do—that is, the factors that determine judicial behavior. In Mexico, many of the studies have focused on the analysis of external factors to explain both the institutional design of the judiciary and the behavior of judges. For example, in the first case, explanations such as the fragmentation of the political system (Ríos-Figueroa, 2007), political legitimacy (Inclán, 2009), or the electoral interests of the ruling class (executive and legislators) (Finkel, 2008) are alluded to, while in the case of judicial behavior, strategic (Cortez, 2014; Staton, 2008), attitudinal-ideological (Sánchez et al., 2011), or ideational (Cortez, 2020; Ingram, 2016b) explanations are presented to understand the decisions of judges.

While we do have explanations that enhance our understanding of when and under what conditions judges make decisions that run counter to the policies and preferences of the executive, we still lack comprehensive knowledge about those who comprise the judiciary. Specifically, we are not well informed about the judges' social backgrounds, their legal ideas and beliefs, how they position themselves within the political system and democratic regime, their affiliations, and their perceptions of the surrounding political landscape. We do not know much about the internal dynamics of the judiciary in Mexico.

Furthermore, despite its evolution since the democratic transition, studies in the field of judicial politics in Mexico still exhibit notable gaps. For example, little attention has been paid to the analysis of intermediate judicial institutions such as judges in district and circuit courts, as well as judges in the judiciaries of states. Most of the studies on judicial politics in Mexico have brought us closer to knowing justices of the Supreme

Court and their relationship with other powers (Castagnola & López, 2016; Castillejos-Aragón, 2013; Ingram, 2016a; Pozas-Loyo & Ríos-Figueroa, 2010; Sánchez et al., 2011; Saavedra 2020). In summary, the studies focused on judicial politics in Mexico have overlooked the internal dynamics of the courts, specifically aspects concerning the sociopolitical origins of judges, their education and professional journeys, the paths they take in their careers, the institutions where they receive training, and the prevailing legal culture they adhere to.

This book provides an account of the characteristics, profiles, and legal culture of one of the least explored political elites in Mexican democracy: subnational judges of the federal judiciary. Based on the data collected in an original survey with federal judges, topics such as where they come from, where they were trained, how they accessed the judiciary, what types of ideas and legal conceptions they have developed, and what their beliefs are about the political role of judges are analyzed. Additionally, in order to recognize their legal culture in the light of controversial or hard cases, their opinions regarding rights and freedoms such as abortion, decriminalization of drugs, same-sex marriage, or the legalization of marijuana are explored.

The research contributes to understanding the judiciary from inside, that is, from the description that judges make of themselves. This book presents a careful characterization of the profile of judges in order to understand judicial behavior from the ideas, values, and beliefs of judges, what they think about the relationship between law and politics, what they believe is their role in the protection of rights, or if they consider themselves political actors with authority to create or reformulate laws from the bench. We will then know the judiciary not from its rulings, but from what they describe and draw of themselves. In this book, judges are given a voice.

Likewise, the argument I develop in this book expands the literature on the importance of internal factors such as professional trajectory, judicial careers, and, in particular, the legal culture of judges. Recognizing the significance of such internal factors in judicial behavior, as highlighted by scholars like Nunes (2010), Ingram (2016b), González-Ocantos (2016), and Ansolabehere et al. (2023), one of the primary contributions of this book is to introduce an analytical framework for operationalizing and measuring one of the concepts that is considered important, but has been less frequently employed in explaining judicial behavior: the legal culture of judges. So far, the literature on judicial politics has been little concerned with defining and measuring systematically the legal culture of judges, despite the fact that this can offer important insights to understand judicial behavior. (Couso, Huneeus and Sieder, 2010) Also, this book pays special attention to the internal procedures that allow for the reproduction of practices and professional rituals in the judicial career, that is, in the internal life of the judiciary. Gaining insights into their organizational structure, career progression, and the criteria emphasized in their evaluations by considering the firsthand experiences of federal judges will offer a unique insight into the internal dynamics of the judiciary. This will address an important challenge in the field of judicial politics in Mexico.

Understanding the judiciary from the inside is essential because it enables us to draw valid inferences regarding the potential impacts of judges' legal culture, their social backgrounds, and professional journeys on the decisions they deliver. For example, it is known that the legal conceptions of a positivist-formalist judge are different from those of a constitutionalist-argumentative judge, so we can expect them to defend the political regime and rights differently, as well as have a different understanding of their role in society and politics. This is of critical importance for democracy and in contexts of democratic erosion, as most of the judiciaries of the third wave of democratizations are independent judiciaries and have constitutional review powers that put them in an unbeatable position to transform the political regime and rights. Thus, this book provides evidence that lays the groundwork for knowing whether judges in Mexico are up to the task of defending democracy and rights or rather legitimizing reforms that undermine them.

Organization of the Book

This book comprises seven chapters that seek to unravel the profile of those who occupy the halls of justice, specifically, the judges in district and circuit courts, and magistrates in electoral courts. Chapter 2 presents the theoretical discussion that has been generated in Mexico—and in other parts of the world—in relation to judicial politics, particularly regarding judicial behavior and the incentives judges have to decide as they do. It accounts for institutional changes (judicial reform) and the explanations that have been provided by the literature for this phenomenon and for the subsequent activism and empowerment of judges. In this discussion, ideational theories in judicial politics are central (Ansolabehere et al.,

2023; Ingram, 2016a, 2016b; Nuñez, 2010). The ideas of judges are fundamental in decision making. The choices they make are based on the law, but also on their legal culture—that is, on their "legal preferences" (González-Ocantos, 2016). Judges have and shape their ideas throughout their trajectory: from law school to their judicial circle or the career they follow in the courts. These ideas do not disappear when they occupy a position in the highest ranks of the judicial career. In this chapter, I contribute to advancing the studies of ideational theories of judicial behavior. To do so, the concept of legal culture of judges is unpacked and operationalized considering three fields of study: judicial politics, the sociology of law, and the philosophy of law.

Chapter 3 is a methodological contribution to the study and analysis of the judiciary. Judicial politics has sought to study the courts and their judges with various methods and research techniques of social sciences. This includes qualitative studies, based on interviews, ethnographies, and analysis of rulings, to quantitative studies based on surveys, databases with votes and rulings, even experiments, and mixed methods. The legal culture of judges and the internal dynamics of the judiciary are phenomena that have been studied mainly with ethnographic techniques and in-depth interviews. In this chapter, the challenges, advantages, and disadvantages derived from exploring the judiciary through a face-to-face survey with judges are presented. The chapter discusses how the data collection process was, the number of judges surveyed, and the strategies that were most useful to open the door of federal judiciary and be able to collect the data with one of the most isolated and hermetic elites of the political system. The main contribution of the chapter is not only to make the data collection and the research process transparent—something that is not frequently done in studies of judicial politics in Latin America (Kapiszewski & Taylor, 2008)—but also to know the variety of techniques and methods that have been used to study the judiciary.

In Chapter 4, I delve into the realm of judges by exploring their sociopolitical backgrounds. How has the judicial family been built? In the study of political elites, it is a common observation that politicians often enter the realm of politics and attain public office through family connections (Montaño, 2017). However, in the case of the judges surveyed, the gathered data indicate that the current judges and magistrates did not enter the judiciary through a family tradition or lineage, but rather their entry into the judiciary represented a change and an upward movement on the social ladder for both the judges and their families. Judges describe their backgrounds as lower or middle class, yet their current socioeconomic status places them among the highest-paid elites in Mexico. In fact, there have been many criticisms of the current government regarding the high salaries that judges in the federal judiciary receive. Therefore, there is evidence of upward social mobility among those who currently serve as judges, which could be linked to their educational achievements and the positions they have occupied, both within and outside the judiciary. The current "judicial family" (judges and magistrates) is an interesting mix of meritocratic efforts, professional networks, and personal commitments derived from the prestige earned by the institution after its reform, something that contrasts with the nepotism that has been observed in the lower echelons of the judiciary (Ríos-Figueroa, 2018), which jeopardizes the professionalism achieved by the institution.

To follow up on judges' sociopolitical origins and professional trajectory, Chapter 5 is dedicated to exploring recruitment and the judicial career. Data are presented on what their route of entry into the federal judiciary was, the trajectory judges have followed within it, their perceptions concerning the operation of the judicial career, and the criteria that matter when vying for higher positions. The chapter begins analyzing the different models of judicial governance that operate or have operated in the judicial systems: the clientelist model, the recognition model, and the professional judicial service model. These models persist as integral components of the recruitment system within the Mexican judiciary. On the one hand, there are still spaces of discretion that become determinant in the success of the judicial career (such as the unsupervised and discretionary entry of secretaries and other lower-rank personnel) and, on the other hand, there are competitive contests (although most of the time only members of the federal judiciary can access them) to select those who will occupy the highest positions in the judicial career (circuit and district judges); finally, the presence of the recognition system for members of the Supreme Court of Justice of the Nation (SCJN) and the magistrates of the Electoral Tribunal of the Federal Judicial Power is verified.

Finally, Chapter 6 deals with the central task of characterizing the prevalent types of legal culture within the federal judiciary. The findings reveal that there is not a singular type of legal culture among judges, and it is not primarily formalist-positivist as one might expect from an elite educated in passive teaching models and characterized by highly hierarchical work dynamics. In Mexico there are judges who have a legal culture that aligns with argumentative constitutionalism, with judges who are willing to weigh up and interpret the constitution to create policies from the bench, without leaving behind a positivist legal culture in which deference to the enacted law and the protection of the status quo persists. In light of these arguments and types of legal culture, the opinions that judges have about rights and freedoms such as abortion, drugs, and the rights of sexual diversity are also analyzed. These topics have the potential to confirm the legal culture of judges in Mexico because, on the one hand, they concern rights and freedoms not explicitly outlined in the Constitution and, on the other hand, some of them have already been addressed and decided upon by the SCJN. This allows us to observe whether the judges' opinions differ (and how they differ) depending on the court's decisions, the constitutional provisions, or the personal values of the judges. It is worth noting that 90% of the surveyed judges indicated that they profess the Catholic religion, which may conflict with the aforementioned rights and liberties.

In this book readers will find a narrative based on empirical evidence that allows a better understanding of the role we can expect judges from the federal judiciary to play in Mexico's political system and democracy. An original analysis of the internal dynamics of the judiciary is presented and as such it lays the foundations for revealing to the specialized and general public the origins, training, trajectory, and ideas of those who until today had been known for their votes and the institutional design of the judiciary. Knowing the judiciary from the inside will allow us to create new valid inferences about judges' behavior in central issues of national political life, such as defending democracy, human rights, civil liberties, and political freedoms, as well as the effective functioning of the rule of law.

Bibliography

Aguiar-Aguilar, A. (2019). *Government and Judicial Politics in Mexico.* Fontamara, IIJ-UNAM, TEPJF.

Aguiar-Aguilar, A. (2022). Understanding the Judiciary from the Inside. The Legal Culture of Judges in Mexico. *Justice System Journal, 43*(4), 576–592. https://doi.org/10.1080/0098261X.2022.2123288

Ansolabehere, K. (2007). *Politics from Justice: Supreme Courts, Government and Democracy in Argentina and Mexico.* Distribuciones Fontamara.

Ansolabehere, K., Botero, S., & González-Ocantos, E. (2023). Conceptualizing and Measuring Legal Culture. Evidence from a Survey of Mexican Federal Judges. *Politics and Government*. CIDE.

Castagnola, A., & López, S. (2016). *The Role of the Supreme Court in Mexico's Democratic Consolidation*. Tirant lo Blanch, IIJ UNAM.

Castillejos-Aragón, M. (2013). The Transformation of the Mexican Supreme Court into an Arena for Political Contestation. In G. Silverstein, D. Kapiszewski & R. Kagan (Eds.), *Consequential Courts. Judicial Roles in Global Perspective* (pp. 138–160). Cambridge University Press.

Cortez, J. (2014). Comparative Qualitative Analysis: The Decisions of the Supreme Court Against the Executive in Mexico. *Mexican Journal of Sociology, 76*(3), 413–439.

Cortez, J. (2020). *Ideas, Innovation and Organizational Change in the Supreme Court of Justice of the Nation*. IIJ-UNAM.

Cossío, J. (1996). *Cuadernos para la reforma judicial: Jurisdicción federal y carrera judicial en México*. México: UNAM-IIJ.

Couso, J., Huneeus, A., & Sieder, R. (eds.). (2010). *Cultures of Legality: Judicialization and Political Activism in Latin America*. Cambridge: Cambridge University Press.

Finkel, J. (2008). *Judicial Reform as Political Insurance: Argentina, Peru, and Mexico in the 1990s*. University of Notre Dame Press.

Fix-Fierro, H. (1996). The Defense of Constitutionality in the Judicial Reform of 1994. *Constitutional Notebooks Mexico-Central America, 19*, 41–57.

Fix-Zamudio, H. (1997). Brief Reflections on the Council of the Judiciary. In National Autonomous University of Mexico, *Mexican Justice Toward the 21st Century* (pp. 139–187). UNAM.

González-Ocantos, E. (2016). *Shifting Legal Visions: Judicial Change and Human Rights Trials in Latin America*. Cambridge University Press.

Inclán, S. (2009). Judicial Reform in Mexico: Political Insurance or the Search for Political Legitimacy? *Political Research Quarterly, 62*(4), 753–766.

Ingram, M. (2016a). *Crafting Courts in New Democracies. The Politics of Subnational Judicial Reform in Brazil and Mexico*. Cambridge University Press.

Ingram, M. (2016b). Networked Justice: Judges, the Diffusion of Ideas, and Legal Reform Movements in Mexico. *Journal of Latin American Studies, 48*(4), 739–768.

Kapiszewski, D., & Taylor, M. M. (2008). "Doing Courts Justice? Studying Judicial Politics in Latin America". *Perspectives on Politics*, *6*(4), 741–767.

Latinobarómetro. (2021). *2021 Report. Goodbye to Macondo*. Latinobarómetro Corporation.

Montaño, M. (2017). Introduction. In F. Patrón & M. Montaño (Eds.), *Local Parliamentary Elites in Mexico: Attitudes and Performance* (pp. 13–24). Tirant Lo Blanch.

Nunes, R. (2010). Ideational Origins of Progressive Judicial Activism: The Colombian Constitutional Court and the Right to Health. *Latin American Politics and Society, 52*(3), 67–97.

Pozas-Loyo, A., & Ríos-Figueroa, J. (2010). Enacting Constitutionalism. The Origins of Independent Judicial Institutions in Latin America. *Comparative Politics, 42*(3), 293–311.

Ríos-Figueroa, J. (2007). Fragmentation of Power and the Emergence of an Effective Judiciary in Mexico, 1994–2002. *Latin American Politics and Society, 49*(1), 31–57.

Ríos-Figueroa, J. (2018). *El déficit meritocrático. Nepotismo y redes familiares en el Poder Judicial de la Federación*. México: Mexicanos Contra la Corrupción y la Impunidad.

Saavedra Herrera, Camilo. (2020). The Keys to the Supreme Court: "Political Fragmentation and Constitutional Litigation in Mexico. *Mexican Journal of Sociology, 82*(2).

Sánchez, A., Magaloni, B., & Magar, E. (2011). Legalist vs. Interpretativist: The Supreme Court and the Democratic Transition in Mexico. In G. Helmke & J. Ríos-Figueroa (Eds.), *Courts in Latin America* (pp. 187–218). Cambridge University Press.

Staton, J. (2008). Formal Theory in Comparative Judicial Politics. *Law & Courts, 18*(3), 10–15.

CHAPTER 2

Judicial Politics in Mexico: Understanding the Legal Culture of Judges

Abstract This chapter presents the theoretical discussion that has emerged in Mexico, as well as in other parts of the world, regarding judicial politics. It specifically explores judicial behavior and the incentives that judges have for their decision making. One of the explanations for judicial behavior is based on ideational theories, emphasizing that judges' ideas play a crucial role in decision making. While their decisions are grounded in the law, they are also influenced by their legal culture. Judges shape their ideas throughout their professional trajectory. This chapter contributes to advancing the studies of ideational theories of judicial behavior. To achieve this, it operationalizes the concept of legal culture based on three fields of study: judicial politics, the sociology of law, and the philosophy of law.

Keywords Judicial politics · Judicial behavior · Judges · Legal culture · Sociology of law · Philosophy of law

Studies of judicial politics in Mexico are relatively new compared to other subjects in the field of political science. The study of politics has focused on topics such as congresses, the presidency, political parties, electoral systems, or interest groups, to name just some of the most recurrent

A. A. Aguiar Aguilar, *Legal Culture, Sociopolitical Origins and Professional Careers of Judges in Mexico*,
https://doi.org/10.1007/978-3-031-52909-2_2

themes in the discipline. This is not surprising, for several political and institutional reasons. The transition to democracy in Mexico occurred just two decades ago. Before a different political party came to power in 2000, Mexico was an electoral authoritarianism (Schedler, 2006) characterized by the government of a dominant party, the Institutional Revolutionary Party (PRI), as well as by a strong presidentialism where the federal executive was the key player around which all political actors and institutions orbited (Carpizo, 2001). In this political context, the courts and the entire justice system were at the service of the president: judges or prosecutors aligned with the wishes of the executive, who controlled appointments, dismissals, and the internal institutional life of the Supreme Court of Justice of the Nation (SCJN or Supreme Court) through its permanent absolute majority in the Senate (institution that collaborated in the appointment of Supreme Court justices) and the overwhelming power of the presidency. During this period, there was no doubt among political scientists that the most important figure to analyze was the party and the absolute authority of the president. In fact, most of the work on institutions in political science focused on studying Mexican presidentialism and its hegemonic party system, and it was only in the early 2000s that studies on judicial politics in Mexico began to be published, in which the political role of the Supreme Court was analyzed. Given the lack of political relevance of the federal judiciary during the authoritarian period, the majority of the research on courts primarily concentrated on the description of written norms, procedures, and legal performance. This type of research was mainly conducted by legal scholars, particularly constitutional law professors.

Likewise, during the years of the hegemonic party, the Mexican judiciary did not have sufficient constitutional powers to confront either the "power of the sword" (the executive) or the "power of money" (Legislature).[1] The judiciary was the weakest branch of the political system (Fix-Fierro, 1999), without a veto capacity to limit the power or to challenge legislative and executive decisions. In fact, judges were protectors of the status quo and their decisions did not dare to contradict the policies of the president. On the contrary, when there were demands of unconstitutionality in a law approved by the executive and the legislative, most of the decisions of the Supreme Court reflected the wishes of the government and ruled against the plaintiffs. Likewise, many justices of the Supreme Court during the glorious times of the PRI were politicians waiting for a better position in the government (Finkel, 2008). This contributed to delegitimizing and damaging the public image of the judiciary and judges among society (Mijangos, 2019) and established the idea that the judiciary was not there to deliver justice, but to protect the political elite. More than 20 years after the transition to democracy, citizens' distrust of the judiciary prevails, but many other things have changed, both in terms of the role that the judiciary plays and in the studies that are carried out about it. The public has witnessed the rise of judicial activism in Mexican politics (Aguiar 2024).

As the political regime accelerated its political liberalization, important reforms affected the performance of the federal judiciary and established the rules to leave behind its traditional passive and politically dependent role. In 1994, institutional changes in the judiciary were fertile ground for the third branch to expand its powers. The judicial reform of 1994 gave the federal judiciary the power to effectively review the constitutionality of laws, which allowed the Supreme Court to control the performance of the other two powers through the so-called constitutional controversies and actions of unconstitutionality. The reform also addressed the historical problem of the political independence of the judiciary (Domingo, 2000; Inclán, 2009). It installed new mechanisms for nomination, tenure, dismissal, and salary protection for justices and a new size for the Supreme Court. In addition, to ensure its independence and accountability, the reform created a new model of internal judicial governance, the Federal Judicial Council, in charge of managing the career of judges (promotions, sanctions, dismissals, and relocations), but especially of independently managing the annual budget of the judiciary and supervising the performance of federal judges. The judicial reform provided the judiciary, and particularly the Supreme Court, with the appropriate legal framework to deploy its power and become a significant actor in the political arena. This reform set up, for the first time in history, a legal scenario for the real existence of checks and balances, and the separation of powers, but also the possibility of having a judiciary with institutional powers to contribute to the democratization of the regime through the protection of rights and the arbitration of political conflicts. At the end of the twentieth century, the Mexican political system inaugurated an era in which the judiciary could potentially exercise its political power of counterweight.

Within this political context, works on judicial politics began to emerge in Mexico. These works have mainly taken the Supreme Court as the unit of analysis and focus on (a) accounting for institutional changes in the judiciary and their effects on the rule of law; (b) analyzing the new role of the Supreme Court in the democratic regime; and (c) explaining the behavior of justices in the protection of rights and in the arbitration of political conflicts. Judicial politics in Mexico has privileged the study of courts from an external and institutional—that is, the works focus their analysis mainly on the relationship of the judiciary with other actors in the political system, whether these are the executive, the legislative, or the media. These works have analyzed the conditions under which judges make their decisions and how they affect the balance of powers, but also how and under what conditions political representatives affect the performance of judges, particularly through constitutional reforms and also through the compliance with the rulings they issue.

In this chapter, I tell the story of the development of judicial politics in Mexico through the emergence and transformation of the federal judiciary on the eve of the transition to democracy. This story begins with works on institutional changes in the judiciary, in particular the judicial reform in terms of political independence, judicial governance model, and judicial review. It continues with works on judicial behavior that have analyzed the Supreme Court from different perspectives, among which are the strategic and the neoinstitutional. From this, I develop a theoretical proposal to empirically study one of the aspects least reviewed by the literature in judicial politics in Mexico and Latin America: the legal culture of the judges of the federal judiciary.

Institutional Changes in the Judiciary

At the beginning of the twenty-first century, there were relatively few studies in the field of judicial politics in Mexico. One of the earliest texts to approach the judiciary from a judicial politics perspective was Pilar Domingo's "Judicial independence: the politics of the Supreme Court in Mexico" (2000). A significant distinction between this study and others conducted on the Supreme Court is that it delved into the Mexican judiciary beyond the formal legal framework, concentrating on its political influence and the consequences it has on the system. Analyzing the judiciary and judges as political actors constituted a valuable contribution in a context where political science primarily centered on the traditional power elites within the system (the president, representatives, and political parties), the sociology of law focused on the interplay between law and society, and legal scholars primarily viewed judges as upholders of legality.

A specialized field at the intersection of politics and law emerged to study the political changes that significantly transformed the role of the judiciary in Mexico. These changes granted constitutional powers to judges, enabling them to counterbalance and limit the decisions of the other two branches of government and allowing them to modify the existing status quo. In summary, political scientists started conducting research on the judiciary as a political institution that, through its rulings, gradually influenced the course of traditional politics in Mexico since the country's independence.

Judicial politics in Mexico began with studies that analyze the most important institutional changes to the judiciary (Ansolabehere, 2007; Ríos-Figueroa, 2007) and continue its development with the study of judges' behavior. The judicial reform of 1994, presented by the last PRI president Ernesto Zedillo, was a key moment for the judiciary as it changed, like never before in the history of this institution, the political-institutional performance of the judiciary. The judicial reform in Mexico included three important aspects: (a) judicial independence; (b) the power of constitutional review; and (c) the judicial governance model. The first two touched on the roles of the justices in the SCJN, while the last one focused on the career of judges and magistrates in district and circuit courts, and administering the budget. Let's begin with the transformations in terms of judicial independence, a central theme of various important works on judicial reform (Ansolabehere, 2007; Finkel, 2008; Ríos-Figueroa, 2007).

The *de jure* political independence of the judiciary was achieved thanks to the constitutional modification of key aspects such as the nomination, dismissal, term in office and the guarantee of a high and stable salary for the justices of the Supreme Court. Following the nomination standards in democratic countries with independent judiciaries, the appointment was left to two actors: two-thirds of the members of the Senate would nominate the justice from a list of three nominees proposed by the executive. Justices' dismissals could only be based on Title IV of the Constitution for corruption or illicit enrichment. In order to guarantee higher levels of political independence, the term of office for justices was established to be different from the term of the executive. Thus, justices would hold their office for 15 years. This would prevent the president from assembling his own court for his term of office, as had happened during the PRI governments. Likewise, legislators granted those who hold the position of justice of the Supreme Court high salaries (the highest among public officials) and established the impossibility of reducing them, with the aim of preventing corruption among those who decide the constitutionality of laws.

With the judicial reform of December 1994, seven male justices and one female justice were appointed, and two of those who had occupied seats on the SCJN up to that point were reconfirmed. The remaining 24 were removed from their positions, being offered early retirement packages (Saavedra Herrera, 2018). For the first time, a Supreme Court was established that would be replaced in a staggered manner after the appointed justice had served a 15-year term.[2] Justices replacements in the SCJN have been carried out in an institutional, regular manner and without major complications since the 1994 reform. Organized civil society, however, has repeatedly criticized the lack of transparency in the process to appoint justices, as well as for a lack of rigor in public hearings when senators examine the candidates who aspire to reach the highest court. In particular, organizations has pointed out that the current rules of the game have led to unprofessional profiles and friendly politicians becoming ministers of the SCJN.

The political independence of justices has also been a present component of the SCJN since 1994. Until 2018, governments of different parties respected the political independence of the SCJN. This began to change steadily from 2018, when a new political party came to power. From 1994 to 2022, only one justice resigned from his position due to political pressures[3] and there was only one effort to reduce the salaries of the justices and judges of the federal judiciary so that their salary is not above that of the president.[4] Despite this, and thanks to the staggered system of appointments and the fixed term of the justices, the pillars of judicial independence remain and we could conclude that Mexico has an independent Supreme Court that is not entirely manipulated to issue rulings that please the ruling political power.

Another sector that was substantively transformed with the 1994 reform was the one related to the authority and power that the SCJN has. Currently, the Court has three mechanisms to review the constitutionality of laws: the *amparo* suit, the constitutional controversy, and the action of unconstitutionality. The first is focused on the protection of fundamental rights, while the other two are focused on resolving conflicts between the executive, the legislative, or subnational governments. An *amparo* suit is a legal instrument that was introduced at the federal level in Mexico in 1847, albeit with significant limitations in its scope, as its effects were restricted to the parties involved. Thus, a law could be unconstitutional, but its application would be regular until each affected party filed and won an *amparo* or representatives decide to change the law. The *amparo* suit is the mechanism par excellence to protect human rights; however, in the 1994 reform its institutional design did not change[5]: "it was not intended for the Supreme Court to be an instrument of defense of fundamental rights (but rather) one of the central features of this reform was to limit the jurisdiction of the court in amparo matters: only those matters that raised the unconstitutionality of a general norm could be worthy of the attention of the highest court" (Magaloni, 2008: 272). This has had important consequences for the protection of citizens' rights and has created a SCJN that does not necessarily protect them (Ansolabehere, 2010), especially when compared with the authority it exercises to resolve conflicts between powers (Ríos-Figueroa, 2011).

A second mechanism that has given power to the SCJN is the constitutional controversies. These already existed before the 1994 reform, but had little scope, had rarely been used, and "had not evolved in almost 80 years" (Mijangos, 2019: 205). That is, despite the fact that the SCJN was formally recognized as a constitutional court, the Mexican court did not have enough powers to declare, *erga omnes*, the unconstitutionality of a law (Mijangos, 2019). The reform presented by President Zedillo revitalized the constitutional controversies and, along with changes in terms of political independence, granted unprecedented power to the SCJN to limit and control the executive and the legislative, and to bolster the separation of powers.

Constitutional controversies are a mechanism of constitutional control that is presented before the SCJN and aim to resolve conflicts between states and the federation, between states, between the federation and municipalities, between municipalities, between autonomous constitutional bodies (federal or local), and the legislative power or (executive, federal or local), due to the invasion of competencies as indicated by the Constitution. They can only be filed by these entities when an enacted law or act invades their powers and sphere of competence. The decision of the SCJN in a constitutional controversy will have general effects when it is approved by at least eight justices of the 11 who occupy a seat in the SCJN (Article 105, Mexican Constitution) and only when it is challenged by a superior entity (for example, the federation against a state). However, if the challenge comes from a lower entity (for example, from a municipality against a state or the federation), it will only have effects between the parties. As can be seen, despite having more authority, the political parties in the legislative chose to continue limiting the power that the SCJN could exert by establishing a supermajority of votes from constitutional judges, but also by establishing a political hierarchy among the parts for the Court's decision to have general effects.

On the other hand, actions of unconstitutionality seek to determine whether a law issued by the federal congress or the state legislatures is constitutional—that is, it seeks to ensure that a lower norm does not violate constitutional principles. They can be filed by 33% of the representatives in the legislative power, political parties against electoral laws, the head of the Attorney General's Office and human rights commissions before the Supreme Court (art. 105 Mexican Constitution). If the vote of at least eight justices is not gathered, the effect of the resolution for action of unconstitutionality will be the validity of the norm; if eight votes are obtained, then the general nullity of the rule is declared due to its unconstitutionality. This type of instrument has been used especially by political parties and by the Attorney General's Office to review the constitutionality of laws on electoral and fiscal matters (López-Ayllón & Valladares, 2009).

With these two instruments, the judiciary experienced for the first time the possibility of setting limits and controlling government authorities through its power of judicial review. However, the use of these resources was not so immediate or numerous (see Graph 2.1)—that is, the constitutional changes *de jure* took a couple of years to be put into practice and reveal the empowerment that the SCJN had acquired with the reform.

Graph 2.1 and empirical studies that focus on the analysis of these instruments and the new power of the SCJN (Finkel, 2008; Ríos-Figueroa, 2007; Sánchez et al., 2011) show that justices began to feel more comfortable and issued decisions declaring laws and acts unconstitutional when political power was fragmented and Mexico experienced, for the first time, divided governments (1997) and political alternation in the presidency (2000).

Another of the substantive changes brought about by the 1994 judicial reform was the creation of judicial governance model in charge of managing and organizing human and material resources of the federal judiciary. Before the reform, justices of the SCJN had absolute control over who accessed to the different ranks of the federal judiciary, from district court secretaries and clerks to collegiate court magistrates. Nominations to those positions were made by justices. There was a

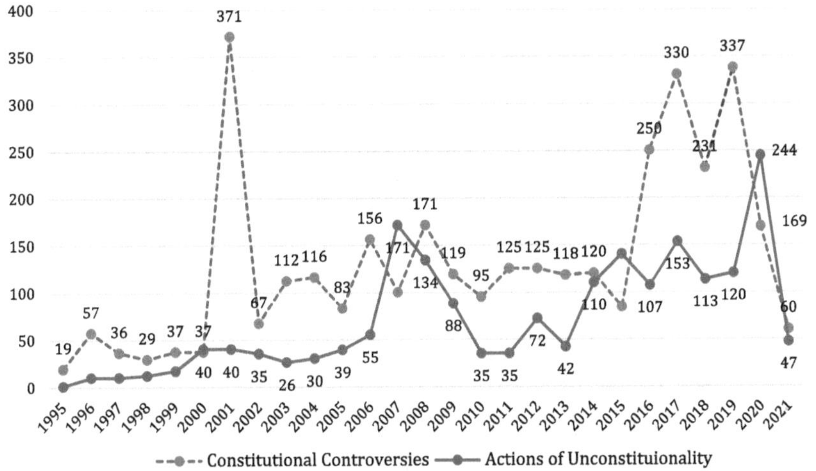

Graph 2.1 Constitutional controversies and actions of unconstitutionality resolved per year, 1995–2021 (*Source* SJCN, Constitutional controversies and actions of unconstitutionality resolved by the Plenary)

"Gentlemen's pact" (Pozas-Loyo & Ríos-Figueroa, 2018). There were no contests or exams to take a position: the judicial family was built on the basis of friendship, family, or relationships within the judiciary.

The judicial reform of 1994 introduced a substantive change in the way judges are selected and how the resources of the judiciary are managed. As a first point, and following the European model of judicial organization, the Federal Judicial Council (CJF) was created. This model of judicial governance was independent of the three branches and was integrated by seven members. Its main task was to oversee and administer the judiciary. Originally, this body was made up of two members appointed by the legislative power (the Senate), one by the executive power, three members of the judiciary chosen by lot from among magistrates from circuit courts and judges in district courts, and, finally, the president of the Supreme Court. However, the 1999 reform returned control of the Judicial Council to the Supreme Court (Fix-Fierro, 2020). Almost like in the best times of the PRI, the watchdog wanted to watch itself again. In fact, some point out that this was a counter-reform (Carbonell, 2000). Since that date, the judicial council is composed of three members of the judiciary appointed by the SCJN, the president of the Court, a member nominated by the executive branch, and two by the legislative branch. This governance management body is always chaired by whoever is president of the SCJN. With this reform, the council lost independence from the Supreme Court and the justices regained partially control of, for example, who enters the judiciary and why. This change had serious implications on the judicial career (see Chapter 4).

The CJF has powers to administer the judicial career and distribute the budget. It is responsible for organizing competitions (public or closed) to select candidates for the judicial career,[6] evaluate the jurisdictional work of district and collegiate courts, as well as the professional profile of magistrates and judges, decide the allocations and relocations of its members, and sanction the misconduct of judges. In short, it provided the judiciary with the basis to develop a judicial career system that, over time, would become one of the best organized in the public service in Mexico. Despite the advances that have been verified in within the judiciary, and as will be seen in the following chapters, nepotism in the judiciary has not been eradicated.

These changes to the Mexican judiciary have been explained from external and internal perspectives. The former focus on highlighting the role of international organizations, financial institutions, development agencies, or specific governments (such as the United States) to push judicial reform (Hammergren, 1998). The latter privilege national political factors (Finkel, 2008; Inclán, 2009; Ingram, 2016). The literature in judicial politics in Mexico has developed three models to explain the 1994 judicial reform: (a) strategic-rational political insurance; (b) political legitimation; and (c) ideational.

The political insurance model starts from the premise that the president and his party gave power to the SCJN because they anticipated that their party (the PRI) would lose future elections. It is argued that the electoral results of the PRI in the past three electoral processes showed a considerable decrease in the vote for this party (Finkel, 2008: 103). This would lead President Zedillo and his group to create a reform that would protect them against future political attacks, in case the party lost even more power in the coming elections. Thus, having an independent judiciary in case the PRI was not in power in the future reduced the risk that the PRI political elites would face if they went into opposition (Finkel, 2008: 31).

The political legitimacy model proposes, on the other hand, that the judicial reform is the result of the need for the president and his party to legitimize themselves before a society that was increasingly skeptical of the results of the PRI in social, economic, and political terms. This model proposes to explain the judicial reform by taking into consideration three moments of the national political context that would increase the political legitimacy of the president and his party by approving a substantial reform to the judiciary: (1) the presidential campaign; (2) the discredit and distrust in the SCJN and the judiciary; and (3) the distribution of power among parties at the subnational level (Inclán, 2009). Thus, it is argued that the president pushed for a comprehensive judicial reform to gain political legitimacy in the face of events such as political assassinations during the 1994 electoral process, the escalation of insecurity, the rise in the perception of impunity, the corruption crisis in the judiciary and the SCJN, as well as the increase in political competitiveness in states and municipalities, where the National Action Party and the Party of the Democratic Revolution had begun to gain citizen support.

Another important explanation for the judicial reform highlights the ideas that the reformers have, their ideological principles, and their programmatic commitments about the "role that courts should play in society" (Ingram, 2012: 440). It is argued that representatives work on passing a reform because they believe in the idea of that the transformation of the judiciary can advance either the quality of democracy or the consolidation of a free market economy. The reformers, or their advisors, are convinced that an independent judiciary with constitutional authority will improve the dynamics of check and balances, the protection of rights, the arbitration of political conflicts, or the confidence in investments and the development of a market economy.

These three explanations have been the most used in the literature in judicial politics in Mexico to account for the incentives that allowed, in an environment still controlled by a hegemonic party, the political actors to grant political power to the judiciary and, consequently, lay the foundations for the transformation of the judges' behavior in their rulings.

Judicial Behavior

Another important set of literature in judicial politics in Mexico is related to explanations of judicial behavior—that is, the incentives that judges have to guide their decisions in one direction and not another. For example, why do judges use their power to settle political conflicts, but not to protect rights? Under what conditions do judges issue rulings against those who govern? Why do judges expand the power of the SCJN? The literature in judicial politics has developed various explanations for the behavior of judges, such as the legalist model, the attitudinal-ideological model, the rational-neoinstitutionalist strategic model, and the ideational or legal culture model (Aguiar-Aguilar, 2019). It is worth noting that in Mexico, but also in other Latin American countries, and especially in the United States, the decisions of judges have been predominantly studied following the rational strategic model.

Strategic explanations consider that the interests and preferences of judges, their peers, and the actors they consider the most important in the political system determine judicial behavior. Theories of strategic behavior point out that "judges are strategic actors who know that their ability to achieve their goals depends on the consideration they give to the preferences of other actors, the choices they expect others to make and the institutional context in which they act" (Epstein & Knight, 1998: 10). This model is also known as the separation of powers model, because judges calculate when to expand or retract the power of the Court, depending on institutional changes, particularly in the balance of powers between the executive and the legislative, as this affects their coordination (Chávez, 2004; Ferejohn, 2002; Ríos-Figueroa, 2007; Staton, 2008). Thus, in Mexico, the SCJN began to expand its power and issue rulings against the party in the presidency in 1997, when political power fragmented and the PRI, for the first time, lost the absolute majority in the Chamber of Deputies (Ríos-Figueroa, 2007). Also, the fragmentation of power at the subnational level—the fact that the PRI lost governorships and municipal presidencies—made it possible for the SCJN to become more active and show its authority and power, especially when deciding constitutional controversies (Sánchez et al., 2011).

Divided governments at the national level served as support so that the *de jure* authority acquired by the SCJN turned effectively into de facto authority: justices of the SCJN realized that in contexts of fragmented power, their decisions would not be easily overturned, as any move to counter-attack the Court would require agreement between the different political parties in the legislature and between these and the president, something that becomes more complex in a divided government environment. In fact, the SCJN began to consolidate the expansion of its power, issuing more rulings against the executive from 2000 when the PRI lost the presidency (Ríos-Figueroa, 2007), and the new president faced a Court that was fully appointed by his predecessor (Cortez, 2014; Sánchez et al., 2011).

This same strategic-rational model has also been used to explain the behavior of justices in the SCJN when they decided to open up to the public and make their jurisdictional work known. To create and increase the legitimacy of the judiciary, and therefore reduce the risk of their decisions being ignored or attacked, the ministers decided to increase their presence in the public sphere through media strategies that make their work transparent and understandable. Thus, "the public serves as a source of power" (Staton, 2008: 13) and legitimacy for the judiciary.

Likewise, judicial behavior in the SCJN after the 1994 reform has been explained by a "progressive judicial leadership" (Castillejos-Aragón, 2013: 145). According to this proposal, the vision that certain justices have about the role of the SCJN and the law, their practices and proposals to change roles and rituals within the judiciary, their efforts to transform the dynamics of the relationship with the other two powers, as well as "pedagogical campaigns" to build active relationships with the media, civil society, and the general public help to explain why the court becomes politically active in matters of rights protection. This explanation considers aspects of the internal dynamics of the judiciary, as does the ideational or legal culture model.

One of the least privileged explanations in the studies of judicial politics in Mexico, but also in other countries, is the one related to the ideational model or the legal culture of judges (Cortez, 2020; Couso, Huneeus, & Sieder, 2010; Hilbink, 2007; Ingram, 2016; Nunes, 2010). Despite this, several researches consider it important to complement the weaknesses of other explanations of judicial behavior, including the strategic one (Aguiar-Aguilar, 2022; González-Ocantos, 2016; Sánchez et al., 2011). In general, studies that take legal culture as an explanation for judicial behavior indicate that rulings are the result of legal preferences or the understanding that judges have about the role the law plays in society or democracy; that is, about judges' vision regarding the legitimate sources of law, how it should be applied, interpreted, reasoned, and justified (González-Ocantos, 2016), but also the ideas that judges have about the relationship between law and morality, and law and politics. Thus, for example, it has been shown that, in the years following the judicial reform of 1994, justices in the SCJN differed in their rulings because they saw the role of law differently: some, like Justice Genaro Góngora, were more interpretivist, while Justice José de Jesús Gudiño was consistently more legalistic (Sánchez et al., 2011: 210–211). The arguments of the interpretivists aimed to expand the powers of the court via their interpretation in cases where constitutional principles were violated, while the legalists pointed out that justices had limited constitutional powers to review such violations and that it was excessive to want to change the law enacted by representatives.

Close to this ideational model are the contributions made by the sociology of law and, although judicial behavior is not evaluated in these works, they consider it crucial to analyze the judiciary from the inside and to better understand the ideas judges have about the law (Ansolabehere, 2008: 332), particularly because we would see different types of rulings depending on whether a judge has a legalistic or a constitutionalist profile. The expectations here are that a legalistic judge will tend to strictly apply the law because more than an interpreter of the constitution, he is "the mouth of the law," while a judge of a more constitutionalist vision will tend to be more active and, based on the interpretation, to expand rights and power of the SCJN.

The argument I develop in this book broadens the reflection on the importance of internal factors such as social origins, professional trajectory, judicial career, and, in particular, the legal culture of judges. One of the main problems that have been pointed out by literature in sociology of law and judicial politics is that legal culture is very nebulous concept. In the next section, I focus on unraveling the concept of legal culture to make it observable and measurable.

The Legal Culture of Judges: A Theoretical and Empirical Measurement Proposal[7]

Resorting to the concept of legal culture is like venturing into a forest full of fog. For some scholars, legal culture refers to how the legal system and legal institutions perform their duties. For others, legal culture is more related to the perceptions and expectations that citizens have regarding the law and justice sector institutions, especially in terms of how, when, and why they decide to resort to these institutions.

Scholars in comparative politics and law agree that legal culture is a difficult concept to define and, above all, operationalize and measure (Gibson & Caldeira, 1996). Some even argue that little can be expected from its explanatory power because it is a nebulous, incoherent, and amorphous concept (Cotterrell, 1997; Couso et al., 2010). However,

Lawrence M. Friedman (1997) argues that we cannot stop studying or working with the concept because legal culture can reveal significant aspects of how the law and legal systems function in practice. For example, the concept of legal culture has the potential to shed light and contribute to explaining why despite having institutional designs that favor the protection of rights, some judges play a more active and assertive role in such protection than others. On this subject, the works of sociology of law and judicial politics have recognized the need to take seriously, study, and unravel the role that ideas and ideational aspects play in the protection and expansion of rights, as well as in the judicialization of sociopolitical rights (Couso et al., 2010). Therefore, the concept of legal culture can be important to uncover a central aspect of the study of judicial institutions: how and why the ideas, values, attitudes, and legal beliefs of the judicial elites affect judicial behavior.

To nourish and unfold the concept of legal culture and operationalize it, I rely on three different literatures: studies in the sociology of law, judicial politics, and the philosophy of law. The discussion here unites different disciplines, giving content to the lack of theorization and conceptualization that other works in judicial politics have shown when discussing the ideas, values, and attitudes of judges (for more on this argument, see Robinson & Swedlow, 2018). I particularly take up the legal theories developed by philosophers of law as the main source to model the legal culture of judges.

In the literature of the sociology of law and judicial politics, legal culture has been defined as "a repertoire of ideas and behaviors, disputed and constantly changing, related to the law, legal justice, and legal systems" (Couso et al., 2010: 6). Other academics argue that legal culture can be understood as the set of ideas, values, attitudes, beliefs, habits, or opinions that a group of people (judges, prosecutors, law professors, lawyers, or ordinary citizens) share with respect to the law or the legal system (Friedman, 1969; Garapon, 1995; Gibson & Caldeira, 1996; Nelken, 1995, 2004; Pérez-Perdomo & Friedman, 2003).

The discussion here starts from the definitions proposed by the studies previously mentioned: legal culture contributes to understanding how law works in practice and the behavior of legal operators and citizens in general. The attributes of the previous definitions are key to the concept of legal culture, but for the sake of conceptual precision and clearer operationalization, it is important to note that these definitions have different units of analysis. In other words, one can easily and confusingly talk about the legal culture of a country, a region, an epistemic community, a group of judges, or ordinary citizens. Friedman made an important contribution by separating the different legal cultures that seem to have different units of analysis. He identified two types of legal culture: external and internal (1975: 194). On the one hand, there are the elites of the legal system such as judges, lawyers, prosecutors, or justices (the internal legal culture); on the other hand, there are the general social groups (the external legal culture). This separation helps to recognize and address the fact that different groups indeed have different legal cultures (Couso et al., 2010). This work has as its unit of analysis the judicial elites in Mexico, so when talking about legal culture, I will specifically refer to the ideas, values, attitudes, and beliefs shared by a group of judges (Friedman's concept of internal legal culture).

The legal culture of judges is nourished by "common socialization processes ... by virtue of their belonging to a structured organizational environment" (González-Ocantos, 2016: 35–36). For example, during their training in law schools, future judges begin to define and shape the role that law plays in society, learn rituals of obedience to authority, and become aware and respectful of hierarchy (Lista & Brigido, 2002). The legal culture of judges develops further during their work as assistants or clerks in courts, where they follow a kind of "pedagogical process" by internalizing the criteria, style, and protocols of superior judges in drafting sentences, which becomes a central feature of having a successful judicial career (Bárcena, 2018). As subordinate officials in the court, judge candidates learn the values that will later be reproduced in their own courts. Other important places for the socialization of legal culture are judicial associations, professional networks, or academic legal communities (González-Ocantos, 2016). In all these spaces, judges structure their visions and understandings of the role they should play in the political, economic or social arena, and of the role that law has in these spaces. In these institutional environments, they learn the routines, legal practices, and rituals that nourish their behavior and professional roles.

In the literature of judicial politics and sociology of law, several concepts close to that of legal culture can be identified, such as "legal cultures" (Couso et al., 2010) "judicial ideology" (Segal & Spaeth, 1993), "legal ideology" (Ansolabehere, 2008; Cotterrell, 1997), "legal consciousness" (Lista & Brigido, 2002; Silbey, 2010) or "legal preferences" (González-Ocantos, 2016).

Judicial ideology is a concept that has been widely used in the literature of judicial politics to explain judicial behavior. In most works, however, this concept remains undertheorized (see Robinson & Swedlow, 2018: 265). Despite this, when studying judicial ideology, the literature on judicial behavior in the United States focuses on the political ideas and values that judges have along a liberal-conservative continuum (Segal & Spaeth, 1993). According to the attitudinal model proposed by Segal and Spaeth, we can expect liberal judges to rule favorably in cases relating to freedom of speech, women's rights, or minority groups, while conservative judges will rule against. In the same vein, other works on judicial ideology base this concept (also without much theorization) on political ideology, arguing that courts divide along the classic political continuum from left to right: judges with left-leaning tendencies favor state intervention policies, while those on the right vote for market-oriented policies (Basabe-Serrano, 2014; Ingram, 2012; Sánchez et al., 2011). Using a cultural theory approach, other scholars conceptualize judicial ideology as specific values such as order, freedom, and equality (Robinson & Swedlow, 2018: 273).

To intervene in existing conceptual debates, it is important to contrast the concepts of legal culture and judicial ideology. They are different concepts. In this work, I argue that the legal culture of judges is nourished by legal theories (see below) and conceptions of law, while judicial ideology is shaped by the political ideas and values that characterize the political preferences of judges in the continuum of the liberal-conservative political spectrum. For example, we can expect that a judge immersed in an argumentative constitutionalist legal culture will have no problem positioning himself on the left–right political spectrum or showing a preference for a particular political party; on the other hand, a judge with a positivist legal culture will deny having a political preference (even if he has one) because judges are apolitical—they are, to use Blackstone's analogy, "living oracles" who apply the law (1983: 69). Note that within this framework, ideological values may appear associated with legal culture in the following way: positivist judges may tend to make more conservative decisions (for example, to protect only the rights that appear explicitly in the enacted law), but this is mainly because they consider themselves apolitical and believe they do not have the power to rewrite the law; likewise, it is because this type of attitude is valued and recognized in the judicial community to which they belong. Thus, for example, if marijuana or abortion are legalized, their decisions will adhere to what the legislation establishes, even if they are not completely convinced of the rule. In summary, formalist-positivist judges may have ideological values and political positions, both conservative and liberal. Thus, the variables of legal culture would tend to be more or less independent of purely ideological variables.

Now, when studying legal ideology, an alternative—although very similar—concept to legal culture, Roger Cotterrell (1997) places a significant emphasis on the relationship between legal ideology and legal doctrine. For Cotterrell, doctrines or theories of law shape legal ideology (but also vice versa): both "help to constitute understandings and social structures, beliefs, attitudes and values" (1997: 22).

Indeed, the concept of legal culture can benefit from the discussion that prominent philosophers of law have advanced about legal theories and legal doctrines. In recent decades, several schools of thought have developed legal theories that guide and shape the practice of law: "positivism," "constitutionalism *of guarantees*" (also called "normative constitutionalism"), "argumentative constitutionalism" (also known as "post-positivist constitutionalism," "legal interpretivism," or "principled constitutionalism") and "neoconstitutionalism." These paradigms have made their way into law schools and even the legal profession, and have shaped the ideas, values, attitudes, and beliefs of judges and lawyers. In continental civil law systems, legal positivism has been the dominant legal tradition, but in the late 1990s argumentative constitutionalism began to spread. The dissemination and socialization of these legal doctrines have been facilitated by the hierarchical and isolated nature that characterizes the judicial community (Couso, 2005). Note, however, that "judges' legal conceptions do not show the degree of internal articulation that is expected to be found in the works of philosophers of law" (Atienza, 2006: 21). Despite this, they substantively influence the practice of law. Below, I briefly expose three of these legal theories, as they have fed the legal culture of judges in recent decades—that is, judges have been exposed to these doctrines to varying levels of intensity: legal positivism, constitutionalism of guarantees, and argumentative constitutionalism.[8]

Legal positivism emerged as a rebellion against conservative natural law philosophers and legal scholars who claimed that law is only valid when it takes into account basic moral principles and the Law of God. Legal positivists, like Kelsen, postulate that morality and law are separate.[9] Some positivists, like H.L.A. Hart, support this separation, but also argue that there is an intersection between law and morality; however, this connection is only contingent and is not necessary (Hart, 1958). According to positivists, "the existence of law is one thing; its merit or demerit is another" (Austin, cited in Hart, 1958: 596), which means that the validity of the law does not depend on ideals of justice, equality, human dignity, or democracy, but on the law itself. Among legal and judicial communities, positivism has been associated with the idea that the moral values or beliefs of judges should not influence their decision making in order for the principle of legality to prevail, and that authoritative norms (those made by elected representatives) should be the main source in the practice of law—that is, judges should consider only what is written in the legal texts when drafting their rulings, and should avoid letting their own moral values and ideas interfere in the decision through interpretation. Given these assumptions, a judge who has a positivist legal culture will tend to issue rulings against policies and social values that have not been enacted and that represent a radical change to the constitutional status quo, such as same-sex marriage or the decriminalization of drugs.

For his part, Ferrajoli (2011: 24) proposes a "stronger" version of legal positivism: constitutionalism of guarantees. As with legal positivism, the constitutionalism of guarantees also holds that law and morality are separate. Ferrajoli asserts that the constitutionalization of fundamental rights would be enough to guarantee the preservation of both institutions and the rights of citizens. The central argument of this legal paradigm is that the "existence and validity of a norm does not imply its fairness" (Ferrajoli, 2011: 31); it follows, then, that we can have unjust constitutional laws, but they are still valid and must be enforced by judges because judicial decisions "that are not based on positive norms, but on moral principles, are not legally valid decisions" (Ferrajoli, 2011: 32). According to Ferrajoli, judges need no more than the power that well-designed fundamental rights exert in democratic constitutions. Judges should not overstep their bounds: in constitutional democracies, antinomies and constitutional gaps cannot be repaired by judicial activism, weighing, or the interpretation of judges, but by elected representatives (Ferrajoli, 2011: 34). Within this legal paradigm, representatives are the only ones empowered to produce norms and correct normative gaps, while judges are obliged to apply those norms that guarantee the fundamental rights of citizens. In this way, the distinction between the rule of law and representative government is preserved.

Critics of the constitutionalism of guarantees and legal positivism argue that it is misleading to assert that judges should decide all cases (particularly the difficult ones)[10] based solely on what is written in the law or the constitution. Even when constitutions are well designed and defend democratic values, we can find cases where there is no defined rule that can be applied to a particular case. As such, judges must interpret, weigh up, and balance a norm to ensure that a fair decision is made.

An implication of this new version of positivism (the constitutionalism of guarantees) is that legalism assumes an important place in judicial decisions and, consequently, the activism of judges is very limited. If judges defend a legal culture of this type, we will find that judges consider that the law is not subject to interpretation nor is it susceptible to being created by the judges themselves. They will not actively or creatively defend rights because, in doing so, judges could lose their legitimacy. Judges may be in favor of new rights, but if they have not been enacted, they cannot be enforced through rulings.

For their part, the theories of argumentative constitutionalism assert that "law is not only constituted by norms, but also by principles ... It is an activity, an interpretive practice in which ends and values play a decisive role" (Atienza & Ruíz, 2009: 135). Legal philosophers like Ronald Dworkin, Robert Alexi, or Manuel Atienza postulate that law has a clear connection with morality, that is, a fair morality (Alexy, 1994). In other words, an ethical morality that guides judges to choose the correct principle when deciding on a case.

Argumentative constitutionalism holds that, in difficult cases, judges should weigh the norms to arrive at fair and correct decisions: "In difficult cases, judges have to interpret the constitutional principles and values (where terms such as freedom, equality, human dignity appear); in other words, they have to choose between their possible meanings and inevitably have to resort to some moral theory (or political-moral theory) to justify, for example, that surrogacy does not imply any attack against human dignity and does not affect public order [in a given democratic constitutional framework]" (Atienza, 2011a: 81–82). The argumentation and interpretation of law are at the center of principalist constitutional theories because norms are principles subject to weighing and interpretation by judges: "Law cannot be understood exclusively as a system of norms, but also as a social practice" (Atienza, 2009; see also Dworkin, 1986). In other words, law is not only statutes and constitutions enacted by representatives, but also a complex practice produced and transformed by the use that judges and lawyers make of the law. Norms are both authoritative and axiological; thus, "interpreting the law implies in a certain sense developing it" (Atienza, 2011a: 82). If norms are subject to weighing and interpretation, then we can conclude that both the morality and the values of the judges play an important role in the adjudication of cases. Since judges are bound by law, but can let their ideas and beliefs take part in judicial decisions, then we can expect to have judges who favor social values or freedoms that represent a challenge to the constitutional status quo—for example, surrogacy or abortion. An empirical implication of argumentative constitutionalism is that when judges face difficult cases, they resort to the weighing and interpretation of norms; therefore, we can expect to observe creative judges and judicial activism[11] in order to defend or expand fundamental rights.

One of the main criticisms of argumentative constitutionalism is the one posed by Ferrajoli, who argues that the idea that there is no separation between law and morality takes us back to natural law, where it is the truth, not the authority, that makes the law (*veritas, non auctoritas facit legem*). However, he points out that the key principle in constitutional democracies is the opposite (*auctoritas, non veritas facit legem*) (Ferrajoli, 2011: 30). The active argumentation, weighing, and interpretation of judges compromises their legal subjection to the law, and puts at risk values such as legal certainty and equality before the law (Guastini, cited in Ferrajoli, 2011: 47).

The previous discussion shows that the doctrines of legal positivism and the constitutionalism of guarantees share some principles and differ from argumentative constitutionalism in the assumption that norms can be weighed and interpreted in light of judges' morality. We can conclude that positivism and the constitutionalism of guarantees essentially differ from argumentative constitutionalism in that in the latter, the judges play an active role in shaping the law when deciding difficult cases.

The legal theories of positivism and argumentative constitutionalism provide central attributes through which different types of legal culture of judicial elites can be observed. Following "concept formation" strategies (Sartori, 1970), it can be pointed out that the concept of legal culture of judges derives from the *terms* ideas, values, attitudes, and beliefs (of judges toward the law), which in turn are nourished and shaped by *attributes* contained in the legal theories of positivism or argumentative constitutionalism, such as the separation between law and morality, the creation of law, the application of law, or the weighing of principles and values. Thus, taking into consideration the differences between these legal theories, in Table 2.1, I characterize how each legal doctrine is expected to respond to various issues of the daily professional work of judges, that is, issues of rights, freedoms, politics, moral values, judicial activism, and legal and social influences (authority) in judicial decision making.

A judge with a positivist legal culture (PLC) is expected to have ideas, values, attitudes, and beliefs that deny his political role or have a political preference on the left–right spectrum. This type of judge will be in favor of the idea that law, morality, and politics should be separated in order to preserve the principle of legality, judicial independence, impartiality, and even the majority principle of democracy. Positivist judges will be against judicial activism, in particular, shaping the law, weighing up different principles, or taking into account criteria based on their own values, social group values, or the needs of society in judicial decision making. On the other hand, judges who align with an argumentative constitutionalist

Table 2.1 The legal culture of judicial elites

Attributes	*PLC*	*ACLC*
Judges' beliefs about their political role	Disagree	Agree
Judges' attitudes towards rights[12] not guaranteed by the Constitution	Disagree	Agree
Judges' values about showing political preferences	Disagree	Agree
Judges' ideas and values about the creation and not just the strict application of the law	Disagree	Agree
Judges' ideas and values about the use of their creative powers to establish the applicable norm in a case	Disagree	Agree
Judges' attitudes towards the weighing different principles when dealing with difficult cases	Disagree	Agree
Judges' beliefs about the fairness of all constitutional norms	Agree	Disagree
Judges' attitudes towards the use of value-based criteria when writing their rulings	Disagree	Agree
Judges' beliefs about the idea that conventional norms are as important as constitutional norms when making a decision	Disagree	Agree
Judges' ideas about the importance of the values and opinions of social groups when drafting a rulings	Disagree	Agree
Judges' ideas about the importance of society's needs when writing a decision	Disagree	Agree

PLC: Positive Legal Culture
ACLC: Argumentative Constitutional Legal Culture
Source Shapiro (1964); Cotterrell (1997); Atienza and Ruíz Manero (2009); Atienza (2011b); Ferrajoli (2011); Saba (2016)

legal culture (ACLC) are expected to recognize having a political role and will not hesitate to position themselves to the left or right of the political continuum. They will defend the idea that judges should weigh up different principles, create laws in difficult cases, and consider their own values and those of the groups close to the case when drafting and issuing their rulings.

Conclusions

This chapter has systematized the development of judicial politics studies in Mexico and has developed a theoretical proposal to operationalize and measure the legal culture of judges. The first section accounted for the studies that, from an external and institutional perspective, have analyzed the judiciary, particularly the SCJN. The judicial reform of 1994 was a milestone that allowed the power of the SCJN to be activated in order to play a more assertive role in the definition of policies that affect the public sphere, but also to transform the internal dynamics of the judiciary through the creation of a judicial governance entity, the Federal Judicial Council, which has had significant implications in terms of shaping the judicial career of judges and in the administration of resources. Years after this reform, the SCJN became an actor that had to be watched and analyzed, as it began to decide cases of political impact, in which neither the executive nor the legislative had reached an agreement. This reform has been explained in the literature on judicial politics in Mexico from varied perspectives. Some works argue that the reform is result of the uncertainty that the party in government has in winning future elections; others point out that political legitimization factors of those who governed are the main reason for reform, while others point to the ideas of the reformers as the engine of change.

In the second section of this chapter, the studies that have sought to explain judicial behavior in Mexico were addressed. The dominant perspective to explain why justices decide as they do has been the strategic one. Judges issue their rulings taking into consideration not only their preferences and what is written in the law, but also the preferences of important actors such as other justices, representatives, and the executive. The studies in this area have shown that when the PRI began to lose its power (in the chambers, but also at the subnational level), the SCJN's rulings moved away from the policies preferred by the president.

Finally, the third section of this chapter contributed to the advancement of the theoretical understanding and empirical observation of the concept of "legal culture," taking into consideration three disciplines that used to sit at separate tables: the sociology of law, judicial politics, and the philosophy of law. Shaping the concept of the legal culture of judges considering not only the contributions of legal sociology and judicial politics, but also the attributes of different theories of law, allows for a better understanding of how judges are expected to behave depending on the legal tradition that underpins their ideas, values, attitudes, and beliefs toward the law. In this way, ideational explanations are refined and one of the main criticisms raised—that the concept of legal culture challenges a reliable operationalization and measurement—against the cultural or ideational explanations of judicial behavior is addressed.

Notes

1. There were constitutional controversies and the *amparo* as judicial review mechanisms. Both were irrelevant in terms of limiting the actions of the executive (see more below).
2. Transitory article number 4 of the constitutional reform established that justices of the 1995 Court would be replaced in 2003, 2006, 2009, 2012, and 2015. Thus, two persons would retire after eight years, another two after 11 years, two more after 14 years, two after 17 years, and three after 20 years (Saavedra Herrera, 2018).
3. In 2019, justice Eduardo Medina Mora resigned his seat in the court without giving an explanation and after having been initiated, and disclosed in the media, an investigation that accused him of possessing resources that he could not justify by his income. It should be noted that Medina Mora's career was highly questionable, as his profile was more political than judicial or academic. Previously, he had served as the General Prosecutor.
4. In 2018, the austerity policy of the new government reached the judiciary. It should be noted that this wage reduction policy was not directed solely at the judiciary, but at the entire federal public administration. The unconstitutionality of the measure forced many judges and magistrates to file an *amparo* suit to prevent their salaries from being reduced. Despite what is established in Article 94 of the Constitution about the irreducibility of the salary during

the term, some justices of the SCJN agreed to reduce their own by 25% compared to the previous year.

5. The reform to the *amparo* suit was not made until 2011, with the promulgation of a new *amparo* law.
6. After the judicial reform of 2021, these profiles include those of judicial officer, actuary, court clerk, court secretary, district judge, circuit magistrate, study and account secretary at the SCJN.
7. Some parts of this section were previously published in the following article: Aguiar-Aguilar Azul (2022).
8. Among some scholars of constitutional law and judicial politics in Latin America, there has been an important discussion about neoconstitutionalism (Carbonell, 2007; Couso, 2010; González-Ocantos, 2016). This legal paradigm has been attributed, among others, to Luigi Ferrajoli. However, he has denied sharing the postulates of neoconstitutionalism and has urged the legal community to embrace the constitutionalism of guarantees that he himself proposes (Ferrajoli, 2011) and which is described in the following pages.
9. It is worth noting that there are different variants of positivism among legal philosophers. Some assert that there is a strict separation between law and morality (normative positivists), while others concede that there is a minimal connection between them (inclusive positivists).
10. Difficult cases are usually those in which human rights and freedoms are at stake, and in which there is no clearly defined norm to adjudicate or there is a contradiction between norms. On the contrary, easy cases are all those that find a well-defined solution in the Constitution or in other laws.
11. It is important to clarify that judicial activism has a pejorative meaning among legal philosophers like Atienza and Ferrajoli. Both argue strongly against it, even when argumentative constitutionalism (from interpretation and weighing) sows the seeds for its development. Scholars of judicial politics like Martin Shapiro (1963) urge us to recognize that judges should be taken as any other political actor who has preferences, but also the constitutional power to shape law and policy.
12. Abortion, same-sex marriage, legalization of marijuana, and decriminalization of drugs.

Bibliography

Aguiar-Aguilar, A. (2019). *Government and Judicial Politics in Mexico.* Fontamara, IIJ-UNAM, TEPJF.

Aguiar-Aguilar, A. (2022). Understanding the Judiciary from the Inside. The Legal Culture of Judges in Mexico. *Justice System Journal, 43*(4), 576–592. https://doi.org/10.1080/0098261X.2022.2123288

Alexy, R. (1994). *The Concept and Validity of Law*. Gedisa.

Ansolabehere, K. (2007). *Politics from Justice: Supreme Courts, Government and Democracy in Argentina and Mexico.* Distribuciones Fontamara.

Ansolabehere, K. (2008). Legalists, Moderate Legalists and Moderate Guarantors: Legal Ideology of Teachers, Judges, Lawyers, Public Prosecutors and Deputies. *Mexican Journal of Sociology, 70*(2), 331–349.

Ansolabehere, K. (2010). More Power, More Rights? The Supreme Court and Society in Mexico. In J. Couso, A. Huneeus, & R. Sieder (Eds.), *Cultures of Legality: Judicialization and Political Activism in Latin America* (pp. 78–111). Cambridge University Press.

Atienza, M. (2006). *Law as Argumentation.* Ariel Law.

Atienza, M. (2009). Impartiality and the Ibero-American Model Code of Judicial Ethics. *Studies of Judicial Law, 151*, 167–186.

Atienza, M. (2011a). Two Versions of Constitutionalism. *Doxa: Notebooks of Philosophy of Law,* (34), 73–88.

Atienza, M. (2011b, April). How to Unmask a Formalist. *Isonomy, 34*.

Atienza, M., & Ruíz, J. (2009). *For a Postpositivist Theory of Law*. TEMIS.

Atienza, M., & Ruíz Manero, J. (2009). *Para una teoría postpositivista del Derecho.* Lima. TEMIS.

Bárcena, E. (2018). Judicial Reproduction and Legal Culture. The System of Appointment of Personnel in the Mexican Supreme Court. *Oñati Socio-legal Series, 8*(5), 739–759.

Basabe-Serrano, S. (2014). Determinants of Judicial Dissent in Contexts of Extreme Institutional Instability: The Case of Ecuador's Constitutional Court. *Journal of Politics in Latin America, 6*(1), 83–107.

Blackstone, W. (1983). *Commentaries on the Laws of England* (Vol. 1). Clarendon Press.

Carbonell, M. (2000). Judicial Power and Transition to Democracy: The 1999 Reform. *Mexican Bulletin of Comparative Law, 97*, 329–350.

Carbonell, M. (2007). *Theory of Neoconstitutionalism. Selected Essays*. Trotta, IJJ-UNAM.

Carpizo, J. (2001). Twenty-two Years of Mexican Presidentialism: 1978–2000. A Recapitulation. *Mexican Bulletin of Comparative Law, 24*(100), 71–99.

Castillejos-Aragón, M. (2013). The Transformation of the Mexican Supreme Court into an Arena for Political Contestation. In G. Silverstein, D.

Kapiszewski & R. Kagan (Eds.), *Consequential Courts. Judicial Roles in Global Perspective* (pp. 138–160). Cambridge University Press.

Chávez, R. (2004). *The Rule of Law in Nascent Democracies: Judicial Politics in Argentina*. Stanford University Press.

Cortez, J. (2014). Comparative Qualitative Analysis: The Decisions of the Supreme Court Against the Executive in Mexico. *Mexican Journal of Sociology, 76*(3), 413–439.

Cortez, J. (2020). *Ideas, Innovation and Organizational Change in the Supreme Court of Justice of the Nation*. IIJ-UNAM.

Cotterrell, R. (1997). The Concept of Legal Culture. In D. Nelken (Ed.), *Comparing Legal Cultures* (pp. 13–32). Dartmouth Publishing Company.

Couso, J. (2005). The Judicialization of Chilean Politics: The Rights Revolution That Never Was. In R. Sieder, L. Schjolden, & A. Angell (Eds.), *The Judicialization of Politics in Latin America* (pp. 105–129). Palgrave Macmillan.

Couso, J. (2010). The Transformation of Constitutional Discourse and the Judicialization of Politics in Latin America. In J. Couso, A. Huneeus, & R. Sieder (Eds.), *Cultures of Legality: Judicialization and Political Activism in Latin America* (pp. 141–160). Cambridge University Press.

Couso, J., Huneeus, A., & Sieder, R. (2010). *Cultures of Legality: Judicialization and Political Activism in Latin America*. Cambridge University Press.

Domingo, P. (2000). Judicial Independence: The Politics of the Supreme Court in Mexico. *Journal of Latin American Studies, 32*(3), 705–735.

Dworkin, R. (1986). *Law's Empire*. Harvard University Press.

Epstein, L., & Knight, J. (1998). *The Choices Justices Make*. Congressional Quarterly Press.

Ferejohn, J. (2002). Judicializing Politics, Politicizing Law. *Law and Contemporary Problems, 65*(3), 41–68.

Ferrajoli, L. (2011). Principalist Constitutionalism and Guarantor Constitutionalism. *Doxa: Philosophy of Law Notebooks,* (34), 15–53.

Finkel, J. (2008). *Judicial Reform as Political Insurance: Argentina, Peru, and Mexico in the 1990s*. University of Notre Dame Press.

Fix-Fierro, H. (1999). Judicial Power. In M. del Refugio & S. López-Ayllón (Eds.), *Transitions and Institutional Designs* (pp. 167–221). UNAM.

Fix-Fierro, H. (2020). *The Power of the Judiciary and the Legal Modernization in Contemporary Mexico*. IIJ-UNAM.

Friedman, L. (1969). Legal Culture and Social Development. *Law & Society Review, 4*(1), 29–44.

Friedman, L. (1975). *The Legal System: A Social Science Perspective*. Russell Sage Foundation.

Friedman, L. (1997). The Concept of Legal Culture. A Reply. In D. Nelken (Ed.), *Comparing Legal Cultures* (pp. 33–40). Dartmouth Publishing Company.

Garapon, A. (1995). French Legal Culture and the Shock of 'Globalization.' *Social & Legal Studies, 4*(4), 493–506.

Gibson, J., & Caldeira, G. (1996). The Legal Cultures of Europe. *Law and Society Review, 30*(1), 55–86.

González-Ocantos, E. (2016). *Shifting Legal Visions: Judicial Change and Human Rights Trials in Latin America*. Cambridge University Press.

Hammergren, L. (1998). *The Politics of Justice and Justice Reform in Latin America: The Peruvian Case in Comparative Perspective*. Westview.

Hart, H. (1958). Positivism and the Separation of Law and Morals. *Harvard Law Review, 71*(4), 593–629.

Hilbink, L. (2007). *Judges Beyond Politics in Democracy and Dictatorship: Lessons from Chile*. Cambridge University Press.

Inclán, S. (2009). Judicial Reform in Mexico: Political Insurance or the Search for Political Legitimacy? *Political Research Quarterly, 62*(4), 753–766.

Ingram, M. (2012). Crafting Courts in New Democracies. Ideology and Judicial Council Reform in Three Mexican States. *Comparative Politics, 44*(4), 439–458.

Ingram, M. (2016). Networked Justice: Judges, the Diffusion of Ideas, and Legal Reform Movements in Mexico. *Journal of Latin American Studies, 48*(4), 739–768.

Lista, C., & Brigido, A. (2002). *The Teaching of Law and the Formation of Legal Consciousness*. Sima Publisher.

López-Ayllón, S., & Valladares, F. (2009). The Actions of Unconstitutionality in the Mexican Constitution: Empirical Balance of Twelve Years of Exercise. *Constitutional Issues, 21*, 175–211.

Magaloni, A. (2008). Why has the Supreme Court Not Been an Instrument for the Defense of Fundamental Rights? In A. Zaldívar & E. Ferrer (Eds.), *The Science of Constitutional Procedural Law. Studies in Homage to Héctor Fix-Zamudio on his Fifty Years as a Researcher of Law. II Constitutional Courts and Democracy* (pp. 271–289). IIJ-UNAM.

Mijangos, P. (2019). *Minimal History of the Supreme Court of Justice of Mexico*. El Colegio de México.

Nelken, D. (1995). Disclosing/Invoking Legal Culture: An Introduction. *Social & Legal Studies, 4*(4), 435–452.

Nelken, D. (2004). Using the Concept of Legal Culture. *Australian Journal of Legal Philosophy, 29*, 2–26.

Nunes, R. (2010). Ideational Origins of Progressive Judicial Activism: The Colombian Constitutional Court and the Right to Health. *Latin American Politics and Society, 52*(3), 67–97.

Pérez-Perdomo, R., & Friedman, L. (2003). Latin Legal Cultures in the Age of Globalization. In R. Pérez-Perdomo & L. Friedman (Eds.), *Legal Culture in the Age of Globalization. Latin America and Latin Europe* (pp. 1–19). Stanford University Press.

Pozas-Loyo, A., & Ríos-Figueroa, J. (2018). Anatomy of an Informal Institution: The 'Gentlemen's Pact' and Judicial Selection in Mexico, 1917–1994. *International Political Science Review, 39*(5), 647–661.

Ríos-Figueroa, J. (2007). Fragmentation of Power and the Emergence of an Effective Judiciary in Mexico, 1994–2002. *Latin American Politics and Society, 49*(1), 31–57.

Ríos-Figueroa, J. (2011). Institutions for Constitutional Justice in Latin America. In G. Helmke & J. Rios-Figueroa (Eds.), *Courts in Latin America* (pp. 27–54). Cambridge University Press.

Robinson, R., & Swedlow, B. (2018). Beyond Liberal and Conservative: Advancing the Study of Judicial Behavior with a Cultural Theory of Political Values. *Journal of Law and Courts, 6*(2), 263–302.

Saavedra Herrera, Camilo (comp.). (2018). *Art. 105. Veinte años no es nada. La Suprema Corte y la justicia constitucional antes y después de la reforma de 1994* Mexico. CEC SCJN.

Saba, R. (2016). *Beyond Formal Equality Before the Law. What Does the State Owe to Disadvantaged Groups?* Siglo XXI Editores.

Sánchez, A., Magaloni, B., & Magar, E. (2011). Legalist vs. Interpretativist: The Supreme Court and the Democratic Transition in Mexico. In G. Helmke & J. Ríos-Figueroa (Eds.), *Courts in Latin America* (pp. 187–218). Cambridge University Press.

Sartori, G. (1970). Concept Misformation in Comparative Politics. *The American Political Science Review, 64*(4), 1033–1053.

Schedler, A. (2006). *Electoral Authoritarianism: The Dynamics of Unfree Competition*. Lynne Rienner Publishers.

Segal, J., & Spaeth, H. (1993). *The Supreme Court and the Attitudinal Model*. Cambridge University Press.

Silbey, S. (2010). Legal Culture and Cultures of Legality. In J. Hall, L. Grindstaff, & M. Lo (Eds.), *Handbook of Cultural Sociology* (pp. 470–479). Routledge.

Shapiro, M. (1964). *Law and Politics in the Supreme Court*. The Free Press of Glencoe.

Staton, J. (2008). Formal Theory in Comparative Judicial Politics. *Law & Courts, 18*(3), 10–15.

CHAPTER 3

Studying the Judicial Elites: A Methodological Approach

Abstract This chapter offers a methodological contribution to the study and analysis of the judiciary. Judicial politics has sought to examine courts and their judges using various methods and research techniques from the social sciences. These range from qualitative studies based on interviews, ethnographies, and analysis of judicial rulings, to quantitative studies based on surveys, databases with votes and rulings, as well as experiments and mixed methods. The legal culture of judges and the internal dynamics of the judiciary are phenomena that have mainly been studied using ethnographic techniques and in-depth interviews. This chapter uses a survey to unveil the legal culture of judges and describes the data collection process and the strategies that proved most useful in gaining access to one of the most isolated and understudied elites within the political system: subnational judges in the federal judiciary.

Keywords Surveying judges · Judicial ethnography · Questionnaire · Data collection with judges

The judiciary in Mexico, as a political institution, has remained distant and removed not only from the people it has the constitutional obligation to serve, providing effective and expedited access to justice, but

A. A. Aguiar Aguilar, *Legal Culture, Sociopolitical Origins and Professional Careers of Judges in Mexico*,
https://doi.org/10.1007/978-3-031-52909-2_3

also from those who want to study it, describe it, and explain it. The house of justice is difficult to access. But this is not new. The distinctive feature of judiciaries as those in Latin America is "the distancing effect they produce, a distancing that in turn contributes to the deployment of (judicial) authority" (Sarrabayrouse, 2001: 213). As a researcher of the courts, approaching judges and their institutions meant navigating a hermetic hierarchy that does not accept outsiders for dialogue and that distrusts those who want to know it beyond the files in which they wield their decisions. The inhabitants of the judiciary do not accept the idea that the judge does not speak only through his or her rulings, but also through his or her practices, rituals, ideas, or even ideology. Above all, many are still uncomfortable with the idea that the judge is a public and political actor, whose work must be known, disseminated, and scrutinized.

The research project from which this book is derived was designed to understand the judiciary beyond its rulings: to understand who inhabits the "house of justice," what the judges' sociopolitical origins are, what political preferences they have, what is their legal culture, with whom they associate and socialize, as well as what opinions they have about rights and their political independence. I was interested in investigating very little-known aspects of those who interpret the constitution, define rights, and set limits to political power in Mexico. In order to do so, it was necessary to approach the judiciary with empirical methodologies from the social sciences.

From political science, the judiciary has been studied with various research methodologies and techniques, encompassing qualitative studies (*Small-N Analysis*), quantitative (*Large-N Analysis*) and mixed methods. Empirical studies of the judiciary have focused on collecting data (numbers, words, or stories) to evaluate various problems that arise from the actions and decisions of the courts. These studies put together the different pieces of the puzzle to determine, for example, why some courts are more assertive than others. Within qualitative studies, we can identify works based on comparative studies of a small number of cases (Ansolabehere, 2007; Brinks, 2008; Finkel, 2008; Ginsburg, 2003; Guarnieri & Pederzoli, 2002; Kapiszewski, 2012; Shapiro, 1981), longitudinal studies of a single case (Hilbink, 2007; Trochev, 2008), as well as historical narratives about the relationship between the judiciary and politics (Murphy & Pritchett, 1961; Shapiro, 1964; Whittington, 2007). In quantitative studies, what we find is the analysis of a large number of observations that make it possible to estimate the behavior of judges (Boyd et al., 2010; La Porta et al., 2001).

Qualitative studies of the judiciary use different data sources such as interviews with key actors in the judicial processes, for example, lawyers, politicians, activists, jurists, and judges; they also use archives, legislation, structures, and institutional frameworks in which the courts develop their tasks; but above all these studies use the rulings and precedents that constitutional judges write on topics where rights or disputes between political power are involved. Additionally, always from qualitative perspectives, important studies of the judiciary have been developed using ethnographic techniques: collecting stories, routines, and legal practices using participant observation (Bárcena, 2018; Barrera, 2012). What Kim Scheppele calls "constitutional" or judicial "ethnography" is conducted (2004).

On the other hand, the most common data sources for quantitative studies are the rulings and votes of judges on central issues for the separation of powers, as well as surveys and databases that aggregate, for example, the institutional characteristics of a large number of courts or the profiles of the judges. This type of work is characterized by collecting "information about cases or judicial systems (among other things) and translating it into numbers to be analyzed with statistical tools" (Epstein & Martin, 2014: 1). Typically, judicial cases or judges from a country are selected and statistical models (Castagnola, 2018) or game theory models (Helmke, 2004; Staton, 2008) are used to explain judges' behavior or their relationships with the executive and legislative branches.

In recent years, there has also been an increase in works that use mixed methods, in which quantitative strategies are combined, such as time series analysis of cross-sectional data, with qualitative techniques, such as interviews and process tracing (Ingram, 2016a). Mixed methods, also called multimethods, are a strategy that combines "case studies with statistical analysis, qualitative comparative analysis (QCA), experiments or game theory models" (Goertz, 2017: 1) with the purpose of "expanding and deepening the understanding and corroboration" of arguments (Johnson et al., 2007: 123). It is suggested that mixed methods provide research with better tools to describe, analyze, and explain sociopolitical phenomena than the use of a single methodology, whether quantitative or qualitative: "the analysis avoids the pitfalls associated with 'monomethod' or single data approaches, taking the strengths of each tradition to compensate for the weaknesses of the other" (Ingram, 2016a: 111).

Other innovative methodologies implemented in the study of the judiciary are experimental methods and QCA. Studies in judicial politics based on experimental methods are still few and have mainly been disseminated in the United States. This type of work seeks to explain the judicial phenomenon (decisions, judicial legitimacy, or votes) using two groups of judges, one given a specific treatment and the other being the control group (Rachlinski et al., 2006; Spamann & Klöhn, 2016; Strother & Glennon, 2021), to identify the variables that explain the differences and therefore a certain outcome. This type of method will then allow us to know what effects, for example, the pressure of society and the media have on the rulings that judges write, based on the differences in the responses that the judges give in each of the groups. On the other hand, QCA studies in courts use a medium number of cases (i.e. judicial decisions) in their analysis and seek to describe empirical causal relationships and interactions of conditions that explain a certain judicial phenomenon (Castillo, 2016). The analysis of judicial behavior based on judicial decisions is built on the basis of the interaction of sufficient and necessary conditions that explain that a constitutional judge votes in a certain way, for example, against the policies implemented by the executive (Cortez, 2014).

In Latin America, works in judicial politics have been developed from both qualitative and quantitative approaches. Most of them are historical-descriptive narratives about the judiciary and a few works have built their own databases to create inferences and account for the problems of the courts (Kapiszewski & Taylor, 2008). These works, Kapiszewski and Taylor point out, also face the problem that they do not report how the cases (most of the time the rulings) were selected, which can lead to erroneous conclusions about judicial behavior. Despite this, qualitative approaches are the seed that allowed the flourishing of judicial politics in Latin America and to know—from interviews, archives, or judgments—the state of judicialization, judicial independence, and the empowerment of courts after the transition to democracy.

In the case of Mexico, the majority of studies in judicial politics are of an exploratory descriptive nature (Domingo, 2000; Castagnola & López, 2016), but there are also various explanatory studies (Ríos-Figueroa, 2007; Ingram, 2016a). From political science, the judiciary has been studied mainly in terms of its institutional characteristics and its decisions, especially those derived from actions of unconstitutionality and constitutional controversies. For example, Ríos-Figueroa analyzes judgments issued by the SCJN from 1994 to 2002 on constitutionality matters and shows how when power is fragmented, judges tend to write judgments that affect the interests of those who govern, something that does not happen when the power of the government is unified (Ríos-Figueroa, 2007).

The study presented in this book follows both instruments of qualitative and quantitative methodologies for data analysis. It studies the case of the internal dynamics of the judiciary in Mexico, in particular, the social origins, the professional trajectory, the judicial career, and the legal culture of the judges of the federal judiciary. Much of the work is based on a survey with district and circuit judges and electoral magistrates, a database with the biographies of the surveyed judges, with which descriptive statistical analyses are conducted. These assessments are complemented with documentary analysis (reports, articles, books and book chapters) on the subject of the judiciary in Mexico.

This chapter is divided into three further sections. In the next section, an approach to the type of techniques used in qualitative methods that have studied the judiciary is presented. Here I focus on ethnographic studies of the courts, since these works have sought to understand the judiciary from the inside and from the perspective of the legal culture of the judges, a key argument of this work. The subsequent section addresses the various studies that have used surveys as an instrument to know various aspects of the internal dynamics of the judiciary and the judges who inhabit it, their practices, opinions, and trajectories. It also accounts for the fieldwork carried out to collect the surveys with the judges of the judiciary in Mexico for this book. Finally, this chapter concludes by pointing out why it is relevant to study the judges of the federal judiciary and how what happens in Mexico can provide insights to what happens in judiciaries and similar legal cultures, such as those in Latin America.

Qualitative and Ethnographic Studies of the Judiciary

The judiciary has been studied from documents, in particular from the rulings of judges, minutes of sessions of the plenary of the Supreme Court, or the institutional designs (often constitutional) of the courts. From judicial decisions, information is extracted (votes, arguments, and reasoning) that account for the behavior of judges on disputed issues in any democracy, such as the separation of powers or respect for civil, political, or human rights in general. The institutional design established in the constitution or in secondary laws has been also useful to understand, *de jure*, the levels of independence, accountability, or professionalization that judges and courts can achieve, but they have also served to estimate the expected level of judicialization of politics, especially from the study of the formal mechanisms of judicial review that the judiciary has at its disposal.

From political science, an additional instrument used to study the judiciary is interviews, which seek to reveal data that documents do not contain. Interviews "allow obtaining information to generate detailed and holistic descriptions, capture various perspectives, or discover different interpretations of the same event" (Kapiszewski et al., 2015: 190). Interviews with key actors in the judicial system have generated evidence to compare what is stipulated *de jure* in legal texts with a *de facto* approach on how the judiciary works in practice, as well as to report and track processes that remain invisible, incomprehensible, or poorly detailed in judicial decisions or other types of documents. Interviews have been an important vehicle for understanding the visions, awareness, and legal preferences of judges and other actors in the justice sector (Cuéllar, 2008; González-Ocantos, 2016), their understandings in relation to democratic politics and the decisions they issue (Ansolabehere, 2008), as well as the interaction between elected authorities, constitutional judges, and their effects on judicial behavior (Kapiszewski, 2012).

On the other hand, but in the same qualitative vein, in sociolegal studies and legal anthropology, judicial ethnography (Scheppele, 2004) has allowed the study of the judiciary from within. This qualitative methodological approach to the judiciary seeks to study "the central legal elements of political entities using techniques that are capable of recovering the lived detail of the political-legal sphere" (Scheppele, 2004: 395). Its goal is "to better understand how constitutional systems operate by identifying the mechanisms through which (judicial) governance is achieved and the strategies by which it is experienced, resisted or revised" (Scheppele, 2004: 391). Thus, entering the institution as an observer is a key strategy, as it allows the researcher to create close relationships with the people who work there, to know in detail their stories, practices, and ideas through interaction with different actors (study and account secretaries, judges, clerks, bailiffs, and judicial officers) in order to obtain their point of view of the judicial world and practice.

Ethnography has made its way into the field of court studies (Bárcena, 2018; Barrera, 2012; Garapon, 1997; Latour, 2010; Verzelloni, 2012) to elucidate how rules operate in the court's everyday life, understand the effects of institutional and hierarchical spaces of justice, as well as to know the beliefs, ideas, and attitudes of judges to opt for that job and develop a career in it or to choose certain arguments and not others when writing their rulings. From judicial ethnography, the researcher immerses in the contextual and "experiential" character of the courts and judges using anthropological instruments such as in-depth and semi-structured interviews, archive analysis, and participant observation that reveal "experiences lived by the narrator, remembered, interpreted, connected and in which there are other actors" (Lindón, 1999: 298) and that make it possible to build a narrative to explore how that experience or point of view shapes the way in which judges decide.

Judicial ethnographies have constructed deep and detailed descriptions of the work of judges and life within the courts, capturing the work culture that is breathed, the practices that are exercised, and the symbols and routines that are important in the judiciary from seeing and experiencing the judicial world "on stage" (Barrera, 2012; Latour, 2010). Thus, the ethnography of the judiciary has provided an understanding of aspects such as who really writes the judgments, distinctive styles when judging, how dialogue is achieved and support for a project is obtained, what behaviors and attitudes define success in the judicial career, where legal knowledge and the arguments that judges use in their judgments originate, or how roles, hierarchies, and identities of judges are constructed (Bárcena, 2018; Sarrabayrouse, 2001).

The legal culture of judges is an aspect that has been mainly studied using qualitative methodologies such as ethnography. Being a concept that is related to the beliefs, practices, ideas, and attitudes of judges, accessing the inner workings of the judiciary would reveal these aspects through the experience of the researcher in the daily work of the courts, the docket, and the routines of the judges and the court staff. These studies have collected novel data, which would never have been revealed by judicial rulings or any other type of documents, about how courts perform, who judges associate or relate with, and how interactions in court occur. For example, an ethnography of the Supreme Courts in

Hungary and Russia at the beginning of the twenty-first century shows how the daily practices of those who inhabit the court make a difference in terms of how they resolve the demands that are put on the table by the citizenry (Scheppele, 2004). In the case of Hungary, the majority of constitutional judges had an active relationship with judges from other European Union countries, with recognized European jurists, while contacts with those who occupy the legislative and executive branches were avoided in order to maintain the political independence of the Court. European law was harmonized in Hungarian law when rulings were made. In Russia, on the contrary, both the legislative and executive branches had their own office in the Court, annual meetings were organized between judges and political representatives, and constitutional judges rarely met with their counterparts from other countries. Even then, Scheppele points out, very few spoke languages other than Russian (2004: 397–398). The results in terms of rights and judicial behavior were clear: the Supreme Court in Hungary was—at the beginning of this century—one of the most active courts and protector of rights, while the Supreme Court in Russia was characterized by being a more formalist court in its rulings and one that showed deference to political power.

For this book, an approach to the judiciary and to the legal culture of judges using a survey questionnaire was sought (see the next section). Different but also complementary to the works in judicial ethnography, I focused on developing a set of closed questions based on the literature of the philosophy of law that would make it possible to identify where judges sit in the different legal traditions and theories of law, and how they describe the legal culture to which they subscribe. This was not an easy task, as it required knowing the path well in order to, for example, unmask a formalist (Atienza, 2011b). In that sense, a closed question about how a judge describes his rulings on the continuum "weighing of principles—strict application of norms" needed various controls to, on the one hand, avoid the political correctness of the judges not wanting to be seen or publicly judged as positivists or formalists and, on the other hand, understand more clearly if their legal culture approached more constitutionalist or positivist-formalist conceptions.

The Survey as a Tool to Understand the Judiciary

Surveys of judges are not common in Mexico or Latin America. However, several notable efforts can be identified, which have focused on subnational and national judges and have sought to understand the judiciary from within. In the case of Mexico these surveys have centered on evidencing the role of judges in the new accusatory criminal system that was introduced in 2008, as well as capturing data related to their professional training, working conditions, and opinions about the functioning of the justice system (Cortés et al., 2016) but also their legal culture (Ansolabehere, Botero & González-Ocantos, 2023).[1] There have also been subnational surveys with judges to discover the attitudes and professional links that exist between the judicial elites and estimate how this influences the diffusion of ideas to reform the functioning of the judicial institutions and the rule of law (Ingram, 2016b), but also to know the organizational and managing challenges of state judiciaries (Concha Cantú & Caballero Juárez, 2001). On the other hand, in Latin America, there have been seminal projects to discover the social origins, recruitment, and professional profile of federal judges in Brazil, as well as their attitudes and opinions about the role of the judiciary in the face of political and social problems (Werneck et al., 1997: 18–19). Also noteworthy in Latin America is the survey of Bolivian judges in which the opinions of judges were explored regarding judicial independence, their professional values, their judicial career, the material resources of the courts, as well as their evaluations around the criminal reform that introduced the accusatory system (Pérez-Liñán et al., 2006).

Judges are a difficult population to survey. They are hard to contact or to convince to talk to outsiders, and their number in relation to the population is small. Sampling, identifying, contacting, convincing, and interviewing are conventional steps in many surveys. Difficult-to-survey populations are groups of people among whom these attributes or a combination of them are usually hard to achieve (Smith, 2014; Tourangeau, 2014: 3). We can think of groups of undocumented immigrants, people living on the streets, drug users, and political elites as some of the world's difficult-to-survey populations (Atkinson & Flint, 2001; Tourangeau, 2014).

For the data-collection process for this book, only two steps of the survey were achieved without many complications:[2] the identification of judges and the conducting of the survey. The website of the federal judiciary openly publishes a complete list of federal judges in all Mexican judicial circuits. This list contains the email and phone number of each of the district and circuit courts.[3] There are 32 judicial circuits, each of them largely equivalent to a state in Mexico. With this information, we prepared a data base containing the judge's name, their court and subject matter, phone number, contact person (usually their assistant or secretary), court address, and tracking status.

The first problem arose with conventional probabilistic sampling. The entire population of federal judges was identified, a random sample was selected, we sent an invitation letter,[4] and then made a follow-up call to ask if they were willing to collaborate with the project. We received only a few favorable responses from the selected sample. Most judges did not respond to our first or second communication. Some who responded told us that the judge "does not participate in projects external to the judiciary" or "were on medical leave." Others asked us about the dynamics of the survey and what kind of questions it contained, while others declined the invitation without specifying a reason. Also, there were some who did accept, but never gave us the appointment. In this first stage, we noticed that judges are wary of collaborating with a project outside of the judiciary. Some scholars argue that "socially isolated people" are hard to survey populations (Groves et al., 2000, cited in Tourangeau, 2014: 13). Due to the dominant civil law tradition in Mexico, but also to the (poor) understanding that some judges have of judicial independence, judges are socially isolated people. In fact, during the data-collection period, one of them told us that they generally do not interact with the media, civil society organizations, or other institutions and people outside the judiciary because the public could question their independence and impartiality as judges.

Judges are difficult to persuade. They refuse, for different reasons, to participate in academic projects in which they have to be interviewed or surveyed. Many have serious time constraints and therefore are not willing to dedicate 45 minutes to answering a questionnaire for an academic project. Others believe that information can be misused or are not willing to talk about what they see as "political" topics. However, it is fair to point out that some judges who agreed to answer the survey were very generous with their time. They showed enthusiasm in making their work, trajectory, and opinions known to an external audience so that, as one judge pointed out, citizens can also get to know them from what they as judges think and not only from how politicians or the media portray about them and their jurisdictional work. Thus, even though our questionnaire contained only closed questions, many of them elaborated their answers and provided detailed information about, for example, the socioeconomic conditions of their families, why they decided to study law, or how they entered the judiciary. Some of our appointments for conducting the survey lasted three hours. We recorded this information in field notes, which are also used in different parts of this book.

One of the ways in which we gained access to the judiciary was through what I called "friendly judges," that is, those who received the invitation letter, agreed to answer the questionnaire, and, in the end, suggested colleagues to collaborate with this "non-media and non-political" project, as one of the judges called it. This procedure resembles snowball sampling or chain referral sampling (Lyberg et al., 2014: 87; Tourangeau, 2014: 9). Contacting judges from other judges who responded the questionnaire was key to data collection.

One way that increased our chances of accessing an interview with a broader and more heterogeneous community of judges was to get in touch—always through a friendly judge—with the coordinator of judges and magistrates of each of the circuits we visited. This reinforced our opportunity to increase the number of favorable responses from judges to be surveyed. Through the coordinator of judges and magistrates of the circuit, we were able to deliver the official invitation letter and schedule appointments with great success. Once they agreed to participate, a face-to-face survey was conducted in person or online (through a Skype video call) by the main or associated researcher of the project. This way of successfully accessing the judiciary reaffirms the idea that judges are a "socially isolated" population that responds above all to the call of peers, but also confirms that hierarchy within judicial institutions matters.

The survey was conducted with female and male judges of the federal judiciary in Mexico between December 2018 and July 2019. At the end of 2018, 1,425 federal judges were working in the judiciary (INEGI, 2019). For this task, 71 judges responded to the survey, of which 40.8% were district judges, 36.6% circuit judges, and 22.5% electoral magistrates. Additionally, 74.6% of the respondents were men and 25.4% women, which is similar to the total population of federal judges: 79.9% men and 20.1% women (INEGI, 2019) (Graph 3.1).

At the time of conducting the survey, the selected judges were serving in the following states (Fig. 3.1): Jalisco (30.9%), Oaxaca (18.3%), Puebla

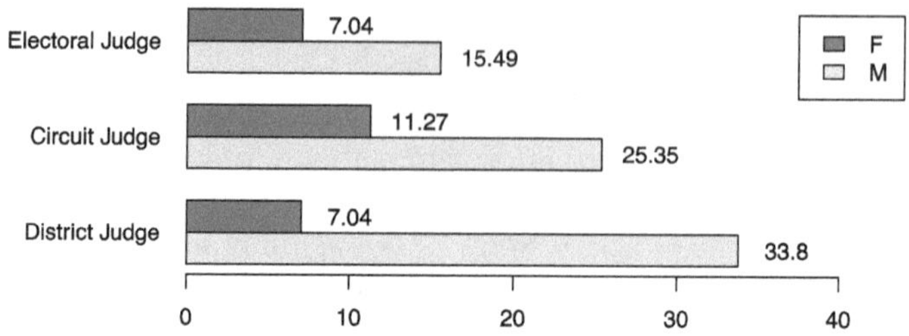

Graph 3.1 Judges' Position and Gender (*Source* Judicial Power Database in Mexico, 2019)

(18.3%), Nayarit (14%), Mexico City (8.4%), Veracruz (4.2%), Nuevo León (2.8%), and the State of Mexico (2.8%). Figure 3.1 also shows the judicial circuits in which the judges have previously served. Transfers and relocations within the judiciary are high for members of the judicial career (particularly for district and circuit judges). Indeed, our sample benefited from the fact that federal judges are transferred to different judicial circuits throughout their careers. The judges in our sample have gained experience in 25 of the 32 judicial circuits in Mexico. The majority of them have worked in at least two different circuits and several of them in more than four circuits (PJF Biographical Database, 2022).

It should be noted that one of the problems with chain referral sampling is self-selection, which leads to a biased data collection, as it undermines random selection and the external validity of the results (Baldassarri & Abascal, 2017: 43–44). The voluntary participation of subjects affects generalization. For example, when surveying judges, those who are willing to be interviewed for an academic project might share ideas closer to argumentative constitutionalism (one of the legal cultures analyzed in this work)—that is, they think that playing an active role in the social and political arena is important for the expansion of rights, the legitimacy of the judiciary, and its jurisdictional activity. The analysis presented here, however, provides new and valuable information about the judicial elites in Mexico. Moreover, since judges are a hard-to-reach elite, it provides more reliable evidence than other forms of data collection, such as the email survey, in which the number of respondents can increase, but only with the risk of not knowing for certain if it was the same judge—and not his or her clerk—who actually responded. Moreover, with face-to-face surveys we had the additional benefit that the judges had the opportunity

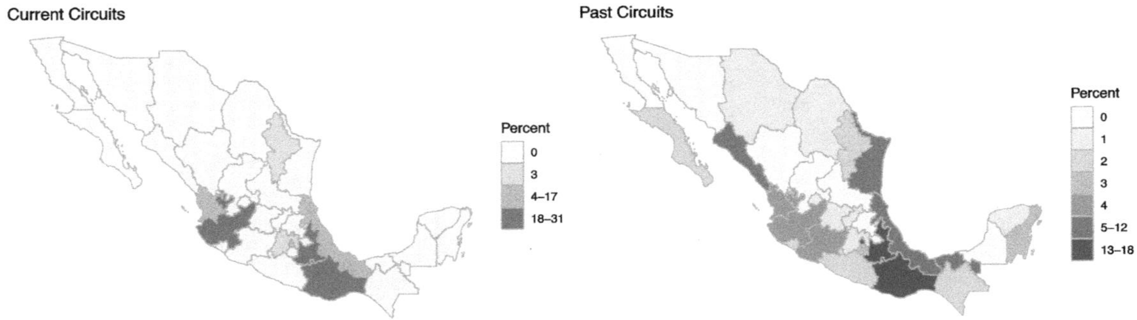

Fig. 3.1 Judges' assigned circuit (*Source* Judicial Power Database in Mexico, 2019)

to provide precise details in their responses, expanding the information gathered, but we also had the opportunity to clarify a question when it was not completely clear to them, thus better capturing their behaviors and reactions.

Unlike other political elites (for example, representatives), judges are easy to survey once they have agreed to participate. They hardly ever cancel appointments, they are on time and ready to take the survey, and there are almost no interruptions during the session. All questionnaires were completed in a single session. This is very different from what is experienced interviewing other political elites, particularly representatives (see Montaño, 2017), who most of the time cancel appointments without notice or interrupt the conversation to attend meetings or take calls. That being said, it is also worth noting that reaching judges in their offices remains a challenge. The so-called "judicial cities" are mostly on the outskirts or outside the city and are guarded by various security filters and barriers. Criminal courts are outside these "judicial cities" and are usually located outside of penitentiary centers (usually far from the city) to facilitate coordinated work between these centers and the judiciary, but making access difficult for people, particularly those with limited resources. On many occasions, the public or private transportation connection to get to these places is precarious, making access to the institution that should make justice accessible complicated. On the other hand, entry to some complexes of the judicial city was also complicated. The building security forces did not recognize the procedure or activity of visiting the complex to deliver invitation letters to the judges or conduct a survey, and on several occasions denied access to the public building.

Once appointments were scheduled with the judges, the questionnaire (see Appendix 1) was applied. This questionnaire is originally inspired by the Latin American Parliamentary Elites Project (PELA), which studies the attitudes and opinions of political elites in Latin America (representatives). Many questions from the PELA questionnaire were adapted to the project of judicial elites in Mexico. Others relating to career and judicial independence were taken from the "Questionnaire to Judges in Bolivia from the University of Pittsburgh and USAID." Other sections of the questionnaire were developed after a careful reading and a thorough discussion of the appropriate literature: philosophy of law in the case of section three; and judicialization of indigenous rights and legal pluralism in the case of section four. The questionnaire contains 167 variables and is organized into five sections:

1. Family and origins: includes questions relating to the sociopolitical origins of judges, such as family economic situation, occupation of the father and mother, level of education of the parents, level of studies of the judges, family political ties, model of legal education in which they studied, and judicial or political networks and associations to which they belong.
2. Judicial career: contains questions about how judges entered the judiciary and how they have been promoted, institutional performance of the judicial career system, the workload in their courts, job satisfaction and their desired future career within the institution, as well as perceptions about insecurity derived from their job.
3. Judicial ideas, legal culture, and legal conceptions: includes questions about the judges' view of the relationship between politics and law, legal preferences on rights and liberties, the validity of constitutional norms, how the law should be applied, what is the status of positive law in decision making, as well as the role that argumentation, interpretation, and weighing play in their sentences.
4. Opinions on indigenous rights: contains questions aimed at determining to what extent judges incorporate legal pluralism into their rulings and use international treaties and conventions, as well as the supreme court's protocols in cases where indigenous rights are at stake.
5. Perceptions about judicial independence: includes the opinions of judges about the independence of the federal judiciary from political, economic, and criminal power.

Once the surveys were collected, the "Judicial Power in Mexico, 2019" database was created, systematized, and cleaned. For data analysis, techniques such as cluster analysis, principal component analysis, and factor analysis (Field, Miles, & Field, 2012) and others were developed to effectively portrait the judiciary from the inside. For data visualization, the R Studio program was used, particularly packages such as tyde-diverse, dplyr, ggplot2, tmaps, cluster, factorextra (R Core Team, 2019; Wickham, 2016), and maps in Mexico (Valle-Jones, 2020).

Conclusion: Studying the Subnational Federal Judges in Mexico

In Mexico, the federal judiciary has been studied mainly by observing the performance of constitutional judges, that is, the justices who sit on the Supreme Court. This work seeks to advance the analysis of the so-called "intermediate judges" of the federal judiciary for a couple of reasons. The first is that we know very little about their origins and trajectories, despite the fact that cases involving human rights protection fall within their courts' jurisdiction that are relevant to advancing the agenda of, for example, minority groups in areas such as indigenous political autonomy and consultation, same-sex marriage, and abortion. The second is that these types of judges are closer to the citizens and reaching them is more frequent and simple for citizens than reaching justices of the Supreme Court. Collecting data on intermediate federal judges allows us to have a more appropriate snapshot of who integrates the federal judiciary in Mexico than if we only look at the Supreme Court. This work joins the studies of the "other judges of the judiciary" and those judges "beyond the high courts" that have been recently developed in judicial politics in Latin America (Beer, 2006; Ingram, 2012; Ingram & Kapiszewski, 2019).

By selecting for study the intermediate judges of the federal judiciary, we were able to broadly observe the results of the reforms that changed the performance of this power in 1994. As we saw in the introduction, this reform radically transformed the way in which the judiciary is organized and, to date, in judicial politics there are no studies on how these changes have been functioning, while legal studies in Mexico have focused mainly on analyzing it *de jure*.

Finally, the selection of the case of the judiciary in Mexico provides us with other methodological advantages to understand the internal dynamics of the judiciary beyond Mexico. The case of Mexican judges is a "typical case" (George & Bennet, 2005; Gerring & Cojocaru, 2016) among the set of judges in Latin American judicial systems, that is, a case that represents a modal trend or that has common values in the structure and conformation of legal systems in this region. For example, Latin American judiciaries share the same civil law legal tradition, mostly the same models of legal education for judicial elites, legal systems with recently acquired accusatory characteristics that changed the way judges used to perform their duties, and a recent wave of judicial reforms that formally created politically independent and professional constitutional courts. Thus, the study on the trajectory, career, and legal culture of judges in Mexico helps to highlight important trends and transformations in the exercise and professional practice of judicial elites in Latin America, where judges traditionally—have often declared themselves apolitical and the mouth of the law (Hilbink, 2007; Ingram, 2019: 184).

Notes

1. Several studies have also used surveys to analyze the judiciary based on the perceptions of judicial officials in general (clerks, court officers, bailiffs, judges, and magistrates), as well as practicing lawyers (see Pozas-Loyo & Ríos-Figueroa, 2021).
2. The data were collected by associated researchers and the author. I would like to extend my special appreciation for the invaluable research assistance offered by Ana Karla González Lobo during the fieldwork. I am also thankful to María José Orozco, Luis Ángel Oseguera, Lorenza Trapero, Iván Padilla, and Rafael Rangel for their research support during various phases of this project.
3. It should be noted that around 30% of the phone numbers were incorrect or the judge was no longer assigned to that court or tribunal. This made contact with the selected population in the first sampling difficult.
4. This letter explained the objective of the project, its funding, the participants, and the strict confidentiality of the responses. It was sent by conventional and electronic mail to each court; in others, letters were sent to the coordinator of judges and magistrates of each circuit, who kindly distributed them among their colleagues.

Bibliography

Ansolabehere, K. (2007). *Politics from Justice: Supreme Courts, Government and Democracy in Argentina and Mexico*. Distribuciones Fontamara.

Ansolabehere, K. (2008). Legalists, Moderate Legalists and Moderate Guarantors: Legal Ideology of Teachers, Judges, Lawyers, Public Prosecutors and Deputies. *Mexican Journal of Sociology, 70*(2), 331–349.

Ansolabehere, K., Botero, S., & González-Ocantos, E. (2023). Conceptualizing and Measuring Legal Culture. Evidence from a Survey of Mexican Federal Judges. *Politics and Government*. CIDE.

Atienza, M. (2011b, April). How to Unmask a Formalist. *Isonomy, 34.*
Atkinson, R., & Flint, J. (2001). Accessing Hidden and Hard-to-Reach Populations: Snowball Research Strategies. *Social Research Update, 33*, 1–4.
Bárcena, E. (2018). Judicial Reproduction and Legal Culture. The System of Appointment of Personnel in the Mexican Supreme Court. *Oñati Socio-legal Series, 8*(5), 739–759.
Barrera, L. (2012). *The Supreme Court on stage: An Ethnography of the Judicial World.* Siglo XXI Publishers.
Beer, C. (2006). Judicial Performance and the Rule of Law in the Mexican States. *Latin American Politics and Society, 48*(3), 33–61.
Boyd, C., Epstein, L., & Martin, A. (2010). Untangling the Causal Effects of Sex on Judging. *American Journal of Political Science, 54*(2), 389–411.
Brinks, D. (2008). *The Judicial Response to Police Killings in Latin America: Inequality and the Rule of Law.* Cambridge University Press.
Castagnola, A. (2018). *Manipulating Courts in New Democracies: Forcing Judges off the Bench in Argentina.* Routledge.
Castagnola, A., & López, S. (2016). *The Role of the Supreme Court in Mexico's Democratic Consolidation.* Tirant lo Blanch, IIJ UNAM.
Castillo, P. (2016). *EU Treaties and the Judicial Politics of National Courts. A Law and Politics Approach.* Routledge.
Concha Cantú Hugo and José Antonio Caballero Juárez. (2001). *Diagnosis on the Administration of Justice in the Federal Entities. An Institutional Study on Local Justice in Mexico.* IIJ-UNAM.
Cortés, N., Rodríguez Ferreira, O., & Shirk, D. A. (2016). *Justiciabarometro. Perspectives on Mexico's Criminal Justice System: What Do Its Operators Think? Survey of Judges, Prosecutors, and Public Defenders.* University of San Diego.
Cortez, J. (2014). Comparative Qualitative Analysis: The Decisions of the Supreme Court Against the Executive in Mexico. *Mexican Journal of Sociology, 76*(3), 413–439.
Cuéllar, A. (2008). *The Judges of Tradition. A Case Study.* FCPyS-UNAM.
Domingo, P. (2000). Judicial Independence: The Politics of the Supreme Court in Mexico. *Journal of Latin American Studies, 32*(3), 705–735.
Epstein, L., & Martin, A. (2014). *An Introduction to Empirical Legal Research.* Oxford University Press.
Field, A., Miles, J., & Field, Z. (2012). *Discovering Statistics Using R.* Sage Publications Ltd.
Finkel, J. (2008). *Judicial Reform as Political Insurance: Argentina, Peru, and Mexico in the 1990s.* University of Notre Dame Press.
Garapon, A. (1997). *Judging Well. Essay on the Judicial Ritual.* Odile Jacob.
George, A., & Bennett, A. (2005). *Case Studies and Theory Development in the Social Sciences.* MIT Press.

Gerring, J., & Cojocaru, L. (2016). Selecting Cases for Intensive Analysis: A Diversity of Goals and Methods. *Sociological Methods & Research, 45*(3), 392–423.

Ginsburg, T. (2003). *Judicial Review in New Democracies. Constitutional Courts in Asian Countries*. Cambridge University Press.

Goertz, G. (2017). *Multimethod Research, Causal Mechanisms, and Case Studies: An Integrated Approach*. Princeton University Press.

González-Ocantos, E. (2016). *Shifting Legal Visions: Judicial Change and Human Rights Trials in Latin America*. Cambridge University Press.

Guarnieri, C., & Pederzoli, P. (2002). *The Judiciary in Contemporary Democracies*. Editori Laterza.

Helmke, G. (2004). *Courts Under Constraints: Judges, Generals, and Presidents in Argentina*. Cambridge University Press.

Hilbink, L. (2007). *Judges Beyond Politics in Democracy and Dictatorship: Lessons from Chile*. Cambridge University Press.

INEGI. (2019). National Census of Federal Justice Administration 2019. Mexico.

Ingram, M. (2012). Crafting Courts in New Democracies. Ideology and Judicial Council Reform in Three Mexican States. *Comparative Politics, 44*(4), 439–458.

Ingram, M. (2016a). *Crafting Courts in New Democracies. The Politics of Subnational Judicial Reform in Brazil and Mexico*. Cambridge University Press.

Ingram, M. (2016b). Networked Justice: Judges, the Diffusion of Ideas, and Legal Reform Movements in Mexico. *Journal of Latin American Studies, 48*(4), 739–768.

Ingram, M. (2019). Interviews. Judicial Politics in the Voice of the Experts. In A. Aguiar-Aguilar (Ed.), *Government and Judicial Politics in Mexico* (pp. 172–193). Fontamara, IIJ-UNAM, TEPJF.

Ingram, M., & Kapiszewski, D. (2019). *Beyond High Courts: The Justice Complex in Latin America*. University of Notre Dame Press.

Johnson, R., Onwuegbuzie, A., & Turner, L. (2007). Toward a Definition of Mixed Methods Research. *Journal of Mixed Methods Research, 1*(2), 112–133.

Judicial Power Database in Mexico, (2019). Available under request at https://aguiarazul.wordpress.com/contact

Kapiszewski, D. (2012). *High Courts and Economic Governance in Argentina and Brazil*. Cambridge University Press.

Kapiszewski, D., & Taylor, M. (2008). Doing Courts Justice? Studying Judicial Politics in Latin America. *Perspectives on Politics, 6*(4), 741–767.

Kapiszewski, D., MacLean, L., & Read, B. (2015). *Field Research in Political Science*. Cambridge University Press.

La Porta, R., López-de-Silanes, F., Pop-Eleches, C., & Shleifer, A. (2001). Judicial Checks and Balances. *Journal of Political Economy, 112*(2), 445–470.

Latour, B. (2010). *The Making of Law: An Ethnography of the Conseil d'Etat*. Polity Press.

Lindón, A. (1999). Autobiographical Narratives, Memory and Myths: An Approach to Social Action. *Economy, Society and Territory, 2*(6), 295–310.

Lyberg, L., Stange, M., Harkness, J., Mohler, P., Pennell, B., & Japec, L. (2014). A Review of Quality Issues Associated with Studying Hard-to-Survey Populations. In R. Tourangeau, B. Edwards, T. Johnson, K. Wolter, & N. Bates (Eds.), *Hard-to-Survey Populations* (pp. 82–108). Cambridge University Press.

Montaño, M. (2017). Introduction. In F. Patrón & M. Montaño (Eds.), *Local Parliamentary Elites in Mexico: Attitudes and Performance* (pp. 13–24). Tirant Lo Blanch.

Murphy, W., & Pritchett, H. (1961). *Courts, Judges and Politics*. Random House.

Pérez-Liñán, A., Ames, B., & Seligson, M. (2006). Strategy, Careers, and Judicial Decisions: Lessons from the Bolivian Courts. *The Journal of Politics, 68*(2), 284–295.

PJF Biographical Database. (2022). Available under request.

Pozas-Loyo, A., & Ríos-Figueroa, J. (2010). Enacting Constitutionalism. The Origins of Independent Judicial Institutions in Latin America. *Comparative Politics, 42*(3), 293–311.

R Core Team. (2019). R: A Language and Environment for Statistical Computing. R Foundation for Statistical Computing, Vienna, Austria. https://www.R-project.org/

Rachlinski, J., Guthrie, C., & Wistrich, A. (2006). Inside the Bankruptcy Judge's Mind. *Boston University Law Review, 86*(5), 1227–1265.

Ríos-Figueroa, J. (2007). Fragmentation of Power and the Emergence of an Effective Judiciary in Mexico, 1994–2002. *Latin American Politics and Society, 49*(1), 31–57.

Sarrabayrouse, M. (2001). Culturas jurídicas locales: entre el igualitarismo y las jerarquías. Cuadernos de Antropología Social, *13*, 205–228.

Scheppele, K. (2004). Constitutional Ethnography: An Introduction. *Law & Society Review, 38*(3), 389–406.

Shapiro, M. (1964). *Law and Politics in the Supreme Court*. The Free Press of Glencoe.

Shapiro, M. (1981). *Courts. A Comparative and Political Analysis*. The University of Chicago Press.

Smith, T. (2014). Hard-to-Survey Populations in Comparative Perspective. In R. Tourangeau, B. Edwards, T. Johnson, K. Wolter, & N. Bates (Eds.), *Hard-to-Survey Populations* (pp. 21–36). Cambridge University Press.

Spamann, H., & Klöhn, L. (2016). Justice is Less Blind, and Less Legalistic, than We Thought: Evidence from an Experiment with Real Judges. *The Journal of Legal Studies, 45*(2), 255–280.

Staton, J. (2008). Formal Theory in Comparative Judicial Politics. *Law & Courts, 18*(3), 10–15.

Strother, L., & Glennon, C. (2021). An Experimental Investigation of the Effect of Supreme Court Justices' Public Rhetoric on Perceptions of Judicial Legitimacy. *Law & Social Inquiry, 46*(2), 435–454.

Tourangeau, R. (2014). Defining hard-to-survey populations. In R. Tourangeau, B. Edwards, T. Johnson, K. Wolter, & N. Bates (Eds.), *Hard-to-Survey Populations* (pp. 3–20). Cambridge University Press.

Trochev, A. (2008). *Judging Russia: The Role of Constitutional Court in Russian Politics*. Cambridge University Press.

Valle-Jones, D. (2020). Mxmaps - Create Maps of Mexico. https://www.diegovalle.net/mxmaps/

Verzelloni, L. (2012). Behind the Judges' desk: An Ethnographic Study on the Italian Courts of Justice. *International Journal for Court Administration, 4*(2), 75–83.

Werneck, L., Rezende, M., Cunha, M., & Baumann, M. (1997). *Body and Soul of the Brazilian Magistracy*. Revan.

Whittington, K. (2007). *Political Foundations of Judicial Supremacy: The Presidency, the Supreme Court, and Constitutional Leadership in U.S. History*. Princeton University Press.

Wickham, H. (2016). *Ggplot2: Elegant Graphics for Data Analysis*. Springer-Verlag.

CHAPTER 4

Who Inhabits the Federal Judiciary? Sociopolitical Origins and Professional Trajectories of the Judicial Elite

Abstract This chapter delves into the world of judges through the description of their sociopolitical origins. How has the judicial family been constructed? In the study of political elites, it is confirmed that representatives generally enter the world of politics and attain positions through family. However, in the case of the surveyed judges, the collected data shows that current judges and magistrates did not enter the judiciary following a family tradition. Instead, access into the judiciary represented a change and upward social mobility for judges and their families. Different to what expected, the current judicial family is an interesting mix of meritocratic efforts, professional networks, and personal convictions derived from the prestige gained by the institution after its reform in 1994.

Keywords Legal education · Judges' social origins · Judges' professional career · Judicial family · Judicial associations

Judges of the federal judiciary are an elite. Some suggest they form an established lineage, often referred to as the "great judicial family," while others cite intergenerational legacies where past generations laid the groundwork for their descendants to become today's judges. The origins

A. A. Aguiar Aguilar, *Legal Culture, Sociopolitical Origins and Professional Careers of Judges in Mexico*,
https://doi.org/10.1007/978-3-031-52909-2_4

of judges within the federal judiciary exhibit a diversity not commonly observed among other political elites. Unlike certain segments of political representatives in Latin America (Barragán et al., 2020), who often hail from families entrenched in politics across generations, the backgrounds of federal judges vary significantly. This diversity underscores the fact that not all judges have familial legacies directly tied to the legal profession. Instead, their paths to the judiciary may be shaped by a multitude of factors, including education, professional experience, and personal aspirations. This departure from familial tradition highlights the dynamic nature of the judiciary and the various avenues through which individuals can ascend to positions of judicial authority.

Currently, there is no data showing the sociolegal profile of those who sit at the courts of the federal judiciary (PJF)—that is, what their social extraction is, if they have political ties, how they were educated, and where or what their networks are. We do not know the persons that issue rulings, decide *amparos*, or refuse to protect rights enshrined in the Constitution and in the international conventions signed by Mexico. We also do not know the social microcosm to which they belong and which they represent and reproduce. Despite this, it is worth remembering that the decisions of the judicial elites have direct effects on the lives of the thousands of citizens who daily claim the protection of federal justice. Additionally, and as mentioned in previous chapters, the PJF has expanded its capacity to influence political and social spheres since the constitutional reform of 1994. It is worth noting, for example, the importance of deciding an *amparo* for a group of people lacking access to health services in a remote community. Like other political elites, judges are key actors that might enable the transformation of society and the political regime; through their decisions, they play a role in shaping the level of democracy of authoritarianism, delineating the rules of the game, as well as overthrowing or maintaining the status quo.

This chapter analyzes the origins and professional trajectory of the federal judicial elite. In the following section, I briefly present a discussion on the study of elites, focusing on judicial elites, aiming to explore the variables that these analyses have taken into account to describe the characteristics and career paths of these groups. Based on the survey collected for this work and a database of judges' biographies constructed from the information available on the page of the Federal Judicial Council, in the following three sections a statistical-descriptive analysis is presented. In the third section, data regarding the social backgrounds of judges, including their parents' occupations, educational levels, the socioeconomic status of their households, as well as the family networks they claim to have in the political and judicial world are all analyzed. The fourth section accounts for the educational and professional trajectories of the judges, the highest level of studies completed, the law schools where they studied, the educational model under which they were formed, the places where they have worked, and the people with whom they collectively associate. In the fifth section, the professional expectations and satisfactions of the judges are described, as well as the constitutional judges who inspire their career and trajectory. Finally, the chapter closes with some concluding remarks.

The Study of Judicial Elites

Judges are among the less studied elites in the political science literature, particularly when compared with the study of parliamentary elites, on which there is a prolific and consolidated research (Ai Camp, 2002; Alcántara, 2014; Barragán, 2015; Best & Cotta, 2000; Dahl, 1961). The biography and professional trajectories of judges allow us to gain a clearer idea of who inhabits the judiciary and to have a solid basis for generating inferences and a better understanding of their rulings, as well as the expectations that are reasonable regarding their behavior. Compared to other political elites, due to the legal tradition in Mexico—but also in Latin America—the judicial elite is one of the most isolated from society as a whole, as it is considered that the opposite would damage the image of independence and impartiality of the judiciary. For example, in a study conducted with judicial elites in Brazil, it is pointed out that judges perceive themselves as "professionals of an isolated subsystem and closed to external influences" (Werneck et al., 1997: 29). Despite this widespread self-perception among judges, it is worth noting that they still belong to political, guild, and family networks (Arellano, 2012), but also to institutions and rules that shape their professional profiles and careers.

In Mexico, there are some studies that have paved the way to know the biographies, professional trajectories, attitudes, and opinions of judges in state judiciaries (see Cuéllar, 2008; Arellano, 2012). These studies describe, using life stories or interviews with judges, who are the people who, on a daily basis, among dockets and courtrooms, sign rulings that affect the rights of citizens. They analyze how judges' access to the judicial world occurs, their vision of law and justice, the characteristics of the "legal consciousness" they develop throughout their trajectory as judges (Cuéllar, 2008), as well as the networks of socialization and recruitment that enable the arrival and professional development of judges in the local judiciary (Arellano, 2012).

In Latin America there are outstanding works on judicial elites that account for the profile of Brazilian judges, their ideas, attitudes, preferences, and inclinations (Sadek, 2006, 2010; Werneck et al., 1997), or in Argentina, where they have studied the family configurations, the educational trajectory, and the socialization and access to the judicial world of federal judges (Donatello & Lorenc, 2017).

The literature on judicial elites has sought to "capture the performance of institutions from the actors' daily routines, without forgetting the social and institutional conditions that weigh on them" (Donatello & Lorenc, 2017: 9)—that is, it seeks to give centrality to the sociopolitical origins and trajectories of judges not only to know them, but also as a variable to explain their behavior. These studies investigate variables such as family origin, educational level, the schools where they studied, religious beliefs, their social links with the judicial world, work experience inside or outside the judiciary, recruitment, access and career in the judiciary, the judges' values about justice, the associative networks to which they belong, their perceptions about the independence of the judiciary, their legal conceptions, and their positions on rights and freedoms, among other variables. The purpose is to discover the judicial world and determine how these origins and trajectories affect political variables such as access to justice, the guarantee of rights, or the quality of democracy. Some of these variables are considered in this chapter to better understand the judiciary from the inside.

The Sociopolitical Origins of Judges

Exploring the lineage of the judges within the federal judiciary prompts an inquiry into their familial origins. Do judges' families constitute a knowledgeable elite, bearing influential family names that have paved the way for their offspring to administer justice today? Understanding the backgrounds of the parents of federal judges offers insight into the diverse socioeconomic, educational, and cultural foundations from which these individuals emerge. The occupations of the fathers and mothers of judges can be classified into three categories: (a) those who are professionals; (b) those who did not undertake professional studies and dedicated to some trade or commercial activity; and (c) those who dedicated to domestic affairs. The fathers of the judges of the judiciary are distributed, almost equally, in the categories of "Professionals" (49.3%) and the one I have named "Trade" (50.7%). The first category includes mainly lawyers, doctors, engineers, accountants, and university professors, as well as school teachers, while in the second are those who were engaged in technical activities, military, merchants, mechanics, peasants, workers, drivers, transporters, merchants, jewelers, ranchers, railway workers, and miners. On the other hand, the majority of mothers were devoted to household duties (67.6%). A smaller percentage (18.3%) worked as store employees, typists in the judiciary, merchants, or bank employees, while the smallest proportion (14.1%) were professionals (doctors or lawyers predominantly) (Graph 4.1).

These findings compel us to limit the idea that the judiciary is a large family built on the basis of nepotism. The data illustrates that a significant portion—50.7%—of the judges' fathers were laborers who lacked university degrees, challenging the assumption that familial connections alone secure positions within the courts. Concurrently, the remaining approximate 50% pursued professions divergent from the legal realm, suggesting a broad spectrum of career trajectories diverging from judicial roles. No

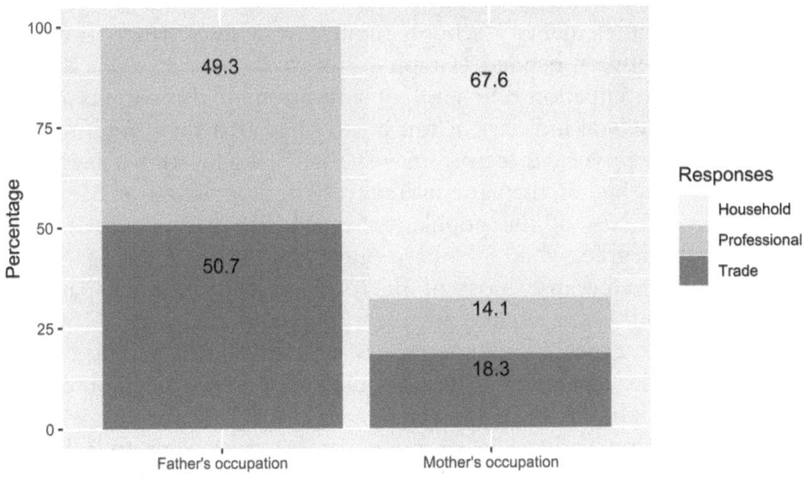

Graph 4.1 Parents' occupation (*Source* Judicial Power Database in Mexico, 2019)

respondent indicated that his or her father or mother served as a judge or magistrate in the judiciary, although some did as administrative officers, typists, and court secretaries. The current sitting judges are the "first generation" revealing an elite arising as a result of social progress (see below). What the data collected in the survey on current judges and magistrates indicate is that they did not reach the judiciary because their father or mother had a long career in the judiciary, or a profession that could influence their arrival at the position they now occupy, as is now the case with the children, brothers, cousins, spouses, and nephews of these judges (Ríos-Figueroa, 2018). In fact, of the judges who did say they had a relative in the judiciary (36.6%), most of the time the relative mentioned was a son or daughter, brother or sister, and to a lesser extent a spouse (Judicial Power Database, 2019). Thus, it could be inferred that the current problem of nepotism in the federal judiciary has developed from the judicial reform of 1994, when judges and magistrates were given the possibility to nominate the staff who work in their courts (see the next chapter).

Regarding educational attainment, 40% of the judges indicated that their fathers completed a bachelor's degree, while about 18% of their mothers did. Furthermore, the prevalence of advanced degrees among fathers was relatively low, with less than 10% possessing master's or doctoral qualifications. Conversely, 33% of mothers completed high school and 28% elementary school, suggesting a discrepancy in educational access between genders (Graph 4.2).

Given the occupation and level of education of the parents of the judges of the federal judiciary, it can be affirmed that their origins are in the moderately privileged sector, since the level of education achieved by their parents is higher than the average of the population in Mexico—currently only 20% of the population in Mexico has a bachelor's or postgraduate degree, while 50% have only primary education—(INEGI, 2020), but also because most of their fathers had a formal paid job (doctor, lawyer, railway worker, merchant, miner, teacher, etc.). However, and contrary to expectations, the judges' parents do not belong only to the most privileged sectors of the population, nor do they come from families with high purchasing power.

A majority, comprising 52% of judges, reported growing up in households characterized by a medium socioeconomic status. This suggests a prevalence of modest yet stable economic backgrounds among judicial incumbents. Furthermore, 25% of judges indicated a medium-low

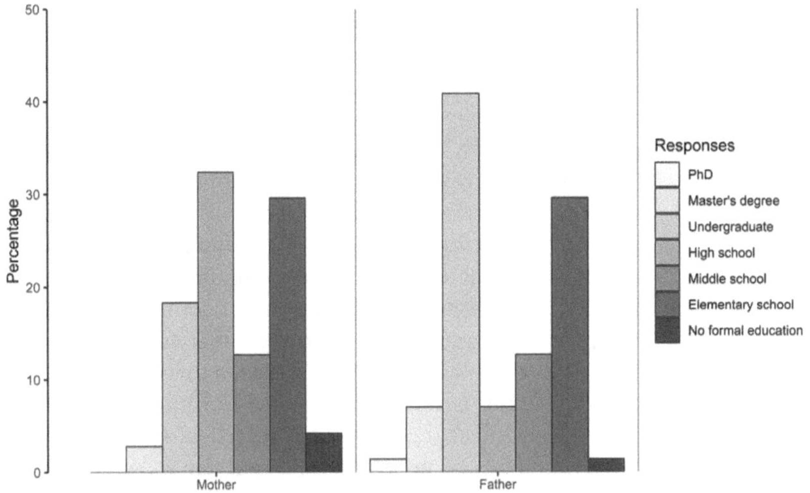

Graph 4.2 Parents' highest level of education (*Source* Judicial Power Database in Mexico, 2019)

socioeconomic upbringing, while 12.7% described their household as low-income, indicating a segment of the judiciary with experiences rooted in economic challenges. Conversely, a smaller percentage—only 9.9%—of judges reported a medium-high socioeconomic upbringing. Interestingly, none of the respondents identified their childhood household as having a high socioeconomic status, implying a notable absence of affluence within the familial backgrounds of federal judges (Judicial Power Database in Mexico, 2019). This finding confirms what has also happened with other political elites, for example, parliamentary elites in Europe, where a rise of the low and middle classes has verified among members of parliaments (Best & Cotta, 2000). However, it also portrays an elite or privileged sector, because in Mexico the majority of the population has been categorized as having a low or very low socioeconomic status, rather than a medium one. To infer more appropriately the socioeconomic status of judges we can also consider the degree of studies they reached (see the next section) which, as a matter of fact, places them in a sector only reached by 16% of the population in Mexico. Thus, as in other Latin American countries (see Donatello & Lorenc, 2017), it is worth highlighting that judges in Mexico represent individuals who managed to climb the social and economic ladder through their careers within the judiciary, leading to their current classification of "high" socioeconomic status (Judicial Power Database in Mexico, 2019). Indeed, judges are among the most well-paid public officials in Mexico.

This emerging "judicial family" demonstrates subtle connections, albeit not extensively pronounced, with the realm of representative politics. Among the judges of the federal judiciary, 23% acknowledged familial ties to individuals who previously held elected office, suggesting a modest yet notable intersection between the judiciary and the political sphere. However, it is important to note that the majority, comprising 76% of judges, did not report any such familial connections to elected officials. Among the relatives of the judges who have been involved in politics we can point out uncles, grandparents, parents, and cousins. Of these relatives who held an elected office, most of them served as mayors, and to a lesser extent as federal congressmen, senators, municipal councilors, or local representatives. Also, less than 10% stated that a relative is currently a member of a political party (Judicial Power Database in Mexico, 2019). These findings confirm the judiciary's distinctiveness from representative and partisan politics, aligning closely with the idea of maintaining a judiciary insulated from political influence—a departure from the era preceding the 1994 reform. During that time, numerous judges harbored political ambitions, contrasting sharply with the current landscape where the judiciary is perceived as independent from political power (Magaloni, 2003).

These are the roots of judges' family in the federal judiciary and the individuals who made it possible for current judges to be able to pursue basic, middle, higher education, and obtain a university degree in law that would be the basis for entering the judiciary and becoming what they are today: judges and magistrates.

Educational and Professional Trajectories

The data concerning the educational backgrounds of judges further reflects their perception of belonging to the middle class. Across their educational journey, from elementary school to the attainment of advanced degrees, a significant majority—over 70%—indicated that they received their education from public sector schools. This prevalence suggests a reliance on publicly funded education systems, aligning with the values often associated with middle-class households prioritizing accessible and affordable education. Interestingly, a shift occurs when judges pursue higher education, such as master's or doctoral degrees. In these cases, most opt for enrollment in private sector universities, often after assuming positions within the courts. This transition underscores the flexibility and opportunities afforded by their professional careers, allowing them to invest in specialized education from private institutions. For example, 45% of the judges who studied for a master's degree did so at a private university or educational center. Of the 20% who pursued doctoral studies, more than half did so at a private institution (Graph 4.3).

In Mexico, the attainment of a law degree is a prerequisite for aspiring individuals to become judges. Therefore, 100% of our judges declared having studied law, with 81% of them doing so at a public university. Public universities are the primary choice for the education of the elite that comprises the judiciary. Expanding on the attained levels of education, the majority of judges, constituting 67%, reported achieving a master's degree as their highest educational attainment. Additionally, approximately 18% of judges held doctoral degrees, signifying an important portion of the judiciary with the highest level of academic accomplishment. For a smaller percentage, comprising 5%, their highest level of completed studies was a specialization, suggesting a focus on niche areas of legal specialization. Furthermore, there were few judges who had solely completed a law degree, indicating that the pursuit of postgraduate education is widespread among judicial circles (Graph 4.4).

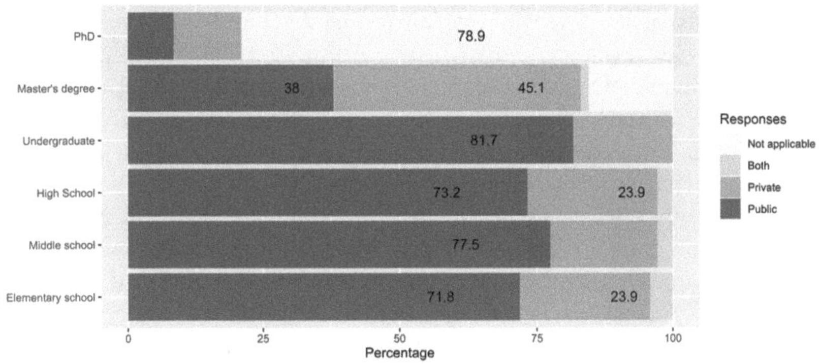

Graph 4.3 Type of institution where judges studied (*Source* Judicial Power Database in Mexico, 2019)

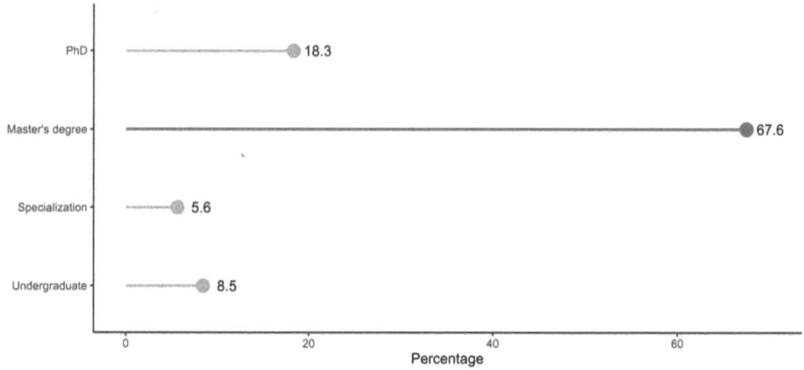

Graph 4.4 Highest level of education achieved by judges (*Source* Judicial Power Database in Mexico, 2019)

As such, we have a judicial elite that has incentives and possibilities to continue studying, updating, and specializing once they have completed the indispensable degree to access a judicial career. Even judges who serve in state judiciaries confirm this trend: "it is no longer enough to have a law degree ... now you have to study a master's degree, a doctorate, you have to be updated" (Cuéllar, 2008: 119). The master's degree is the type of postgraduate degree that federal judges have studied the most, especially those of a professionalizing type (Fix-Fierro, 2020). The specializations they study in postgraduate courses are focused on various areas of law such as Constitutional Law and *Amparo*, *Amparo* Trial, Civil Law, Human Rights, Justice Administration and Gender (PJF Biographical Files Database, 2022). What these data also tell us is that judges have surpassed the educational achievements of their parents. This difference in educational attainment between judges and their parents signals a trajectory of upward social mobility.

On the other hand, the postgraduate training seminars and courses they generally take are offered by public institutions such as the Federal Judicial Council (mainly), the Supreme Court, the National Institute of Criminal Sciences, but also by private universities or centers such as the Monterrey Institute of Technology, the Anahuac University, or the IBERO Mexico City (PJF Biographical Files Database, 2022).

The judicial elite has largely been educated in national and public universities. All the surveyed judges completed their undergraduate studies in Mexican universities such as the National Autonomous University of Mexico, the University of Guadalajara, the Michoacana University of San Nicolás de Hidalgo, the Benemérita Autonomous University of Puebla, the Autonomous University of Guerrero, the Benito Juárez Autonomous University of Oaxaca, and the Autonomous University of Chihuahua—that is, the most important public universities. This confirms the idea that state public universities are the breeding ground for judicial elites (Arellano, 2012). The trend to study at a national university is also verified in postgraduate studies, as only about 8% of the judges said they had completed their master's or doctorate abroad, mostly in Spain, at universities like Alicante, and a smaller percentage in the United States, France, or Italy (Judicial Power in Mexico Database, 2019; see also Fix-Fierro, 2020). In fact, 53% of the judges said they do not speak a language other than Spanish (Judicial Power in Mexico Database, 2019), so the natural places to pursue postgraduate studies are Spanish-speaking countries and, in that sense, Spain is a very recurring reference for lawyers who seek to continue specializing in law. Thus, the judicial elite in Mexico has been formed under a very similar educational model that would tend to reproduce homogeneous legal practices, or lawyers who are made by "the same frame" (Magaloni, 2006: 63), while only a smaller percentage has been able to experience a somewhat different way of studying, thinking, and practicing law thanks to the studies they undertook in other countries. And it is "somewhat different" because the legal traditions of Spain, France, or Italy are not very different from the Mexican legal tradition (Fix-Fierro, 2020: 505), although they have evolved at a different pace after the Second World War.

The educational models influencing the training of judges wield profound influence over their professional conduct, shaping their understanding of law, its origins, its authorities, and its societal role. Research underscores the pivotal role of judicial education in determining the legal conceptions and cultures adopted by judges upon assuming their roles (Aguiar-Aguilar & Torres, 2022). Traditionally, judges have been steeped in educational paradigms characterized by passive methodologies and didactic lectures. This approach emphasizes memorization of statutes and codes, fostering deference towards established authority. However, the contemporary landscape also sees the emergence of the Socratic or case study model, renowned for its active learning methodologies. Unlike its traditional counterpart, the Socratic model places the student at the center of learning. Through the exploration of practical cases and problem-solving, students engage with the law dynamically, moving beyond its textual confines. This model encourages critical inquiry into the creation, application, and evolution of legal frameworks. Moreover, the integration of clinics amplifies experiential learning, enriching students' comprehension of legal principles through real-world applications. By fostering an environment of active engagement and critical analysis, the Socratic model equips judges with the tools to navigate the complexities of law, politics, and society. It nurtures a mindset attuned to questioning, adaptation, and the pursuit of justice in an evolving legal landscape. Thus, the choice of educational model holds profound implications for the judiciary, shaping not only individual judicial philosophies but also their broader legal culture (Graph 4.5).

In Mexico, 57% of the judges indicate that the educational model of the law faculty where they studied their degree was traditional—that is, centered on memorization and of lecture-style classes—while almost 42% pointed out that the model in which they were trained favored the case study model. This changes for the group of judges who have studied a postgraduate degree: 76% claimed that in their postgraduate studies (as we saw, mainly of master's degrees) the educational model in which they studied was one that used active methodologies, focused on the student and learning through the resolution of practical cases.

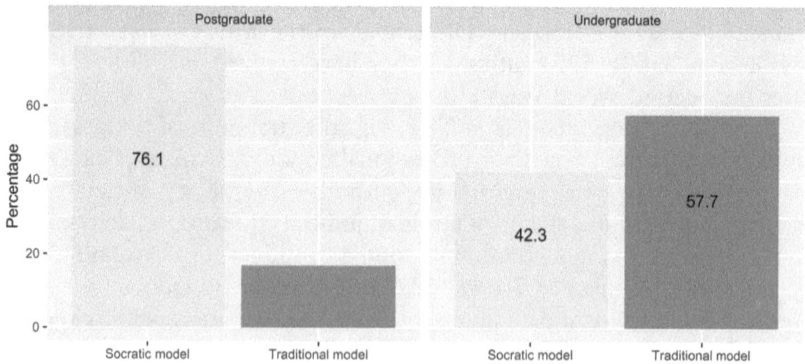

Graph 4.5 Educational model (*Source* Judicial Power Database in Mexico, 2019)

The initial expectation was that nearly all these judges would claim to have pursued their law degree in a program that privileged the memorization and the abstract study of law, that is, under a traditional educational model. However, and despite the evidence from various studies that indicate that legal education in Mexico has been traditional (Magaloni, 2006), many of the judges surveyed who studied in the 1980s and 1990s (42%), and especially those who completed their degree in 2000 or later, claim to have followed an educational model that privileged case studies. These data are consistent especially in the responses of those who studied at universities such as the Universidad Nacional Autónoma de México and the Universidad Regional del Sureste. These counter-intuitive findings may stem from a bias influenced by what judges perceive as "socially desirable", since well into the first decade of the twentieth century, the educational curriculum for teaching law lacked components such as legal clinics or analytical methods for studying judicial decisions. Additionally, there was no requirement for studying other disciplines, such as international law, political science, statistics, or sociology, which could provide a more analytical and interdisciplinary perspective on law. In fact, it has been argued that legal education in Mexico has not evolved in line with institutional changes in the legal field (Fix-Fierro, 2020).

Once they have completed their undergraduate studies, judges have followed different professional paths. A total of 33% claimed to have worked only in the federal judiciary—that is, they are "pure" federal judges who upon completing their law degree (or even before doing so) decided to focus on following the judicial career that began to take shape after the 1994 reform. State institutions (Fig. 4.1) have served as the workplace for 67% of judges. These include public institutions and government at the state level, such as public defenders, prosecutors' offices, state judiciaries, conciliation and arbitration departments, human rights commissions, and the public administration, but also at the federal level like today's Fiscalía General de la República, the National Electoral Institute, or state ministries such as the Ministry of Finance and Public Credit or the Ministry of the Interior. A smaller percentage has also practiced law in the private sector, mainly in law firms, but also in notaries, as free litigants or in banks (Fig. 4.1). These data then reflect the composition of a judicial elite that has built its professional career mostly in the public sector and government. These findings also confirm the traditional view of the professional practice of law in Mexico: law was studied mainly

Fig. 4.1 Judges' Professional trajectory (*Source* Judicial Power Database in Mexico, 2019)

to work in the public sector, particularly in the state or federal public administration (Magaloni, 2006: 77; Arellano, 2012).

The academic sector is another area into which judges venture. As part of their unpaid professional career, around 80% of the judges said they teach or have taught lectures at some public or private universities (Judicial Power in Mexico Database, 2019). Academia and teaching is an activity in which enthusiasm was perceived by some of the surveyed judges and is seen as "a tool to improve their preparation and keep them updated" (Caballero, 2006: 295). In fact, more than 50% stated that when they leave the position they hold, they would like to work on as professors at a university. Other judges said that when they retire from their position, they would like to spend time with their family, become a minister of the Supreme Court, or become circuit magistrates.[1]

In addition to the courtroom, the realm where judges' influence and authority are molded extends to the dynamic sphere of associations and networks. As noted by Guarnieri (2003: 236), these associations play a pivotal role in shaping the profile, trajectory, and influence of judges within judiciary. These organizations serve as crucibles where judges converge to safeguard and promote their professional interests, build their collective identity, and pursue shared objectives that serve to validate their endeavors in the eyes of the public. Judges' associations serve as bastions of advocacy, championing causes that resonate with the judiciary's core principles and values. Whether advocating for judicial independence, budged or wilding influence in the definition of their organizational structure, judges leverage the collective weight of their associations to amplify their voices and effect meaningful change within the legal framework. By aligning themselves with these shared goals, judges not only bolster their own standing within the legal community but also reinforce the legitimacy of the judiciary as a whole. In this survey, more than 90% affirmed participating in some judges' association. The National Association of Circuit Magistrates and District Judges of the Federal Judicial Power is the association that gathers the majority of the surveyed judges. According to the judges, it is the most important in the country.[2] This association emerged in 2001 to consolidate the independence, integrity, and professionalization of judges of the federal judiciary and, therefore, the administration of justice, and has sought to position and defend these interests through agreements, press releases, bulletins, videos, podcasts, social networks and annual meetings. For example, it has spoken out on various occasions to protect both the external and internal independence of judges when they issue their rulings, to question presidential decrees and laws that violate the rights of judges, such as a fixed and irreducible salary, or to criticize the politicization of nomination processes in the CJF. Until 2022, only one female magistrate has been its leader, while 12 magistrates have held this position (ANMJ-PJF, 2022). The association has sought to fulfill the goal of uniting and advancing the rights of the judges of the federal judiciary. In fact, more than 80% of the surveyed judges said they strongly agreed and agreed with the idea that being associated favors the defense of the guild's interests against external pressures, as well as against pressures within the judiciary (Judicial Power Database in Mexico, 2019).

Judicial Profiles, Satisfaction, and Professional Prospects

What are the aspirations of the federal judges? How satisfied are they with their career? Who and what influences their journey in the judiciary? Despite the lack of legitimacy and public confidence in the judiciary reported by various public opinion measurements in Mexico and Latin America, the federal judicial elite is distinguished by being proud and satisfied with working in the federal judiciary and the professional project they have achieved. The judiciary is an institution that the surveyed judges recognize as prestigious, which serves as motivation for their participation within it (see the next chapter). When asked whether they were satisfied with their career as judges or whether they would prefer to practice a different profession, 98% of respondents said they were very satisfied and happy with their judicial career. In fact, an overwhelming majority indicated a desire to remain in the judiciary until their retirement, and several of them indicated the wish to stay there "all their life," "as long as they have the necessary strength," "forever," or until they no longer have "legal capacity and lucidity"; although they also recognize that by law they cannot do so since they are legally obligated to retire at 75 years old (Judicial Power Database in Mexico, 2019). This is particularly relevant with electoral magistrates, as a significant majority express the desire to remain in the judiciary until retirement, even after completing their term as electoral judges. This even applies to those who have yet to successfully navigate the competitive selection process.

The professional aspiration of the majority of the surveyed judges (34%) lies outside the judicial career, although within the federal judiciary: their goal is to attain the position of a Justice in the SCJN. They acknowledge that in order to attain this position, apart from having a well-established career path, it is also necessary to cultivate strong political connections. As mentioned earlier in this book, the appointment of SCJN justices is carried out by the legislative and executive branches of government. A smaller but very similar proportion (32%) pointed out that their goal is to reach the highest position in the judicial hierarchy: circuit court magistrate; this was the case for both the surveyed judges and for some who had already obtained the position of magistrate. In the third position, comprising nearly 20% of the respondents, are judges who aspire to serve as judges on international courts, such as the International Criminal Court or the Inter-American Court of Human Rights. Lastly, a minority expressed their intention to continue in their current role as a district judge, to pursue a position as a counselor in the Judicial Council, or to become a magistrate in the higher chamber of the Electoral Court. It is worth noting that the desire for the latter position primarily emanated from electoral magistrates in regional chambers (Fig. 4.2).

The career aspirations of judges underscore the central importance of advancement prospects within the judiciary (see also Caballero, 2006). It is evident that they are not only committed but are also content with their profession, intending to continue their service as judges throughout the entirety of their careers. Other variables explored in the following chapter

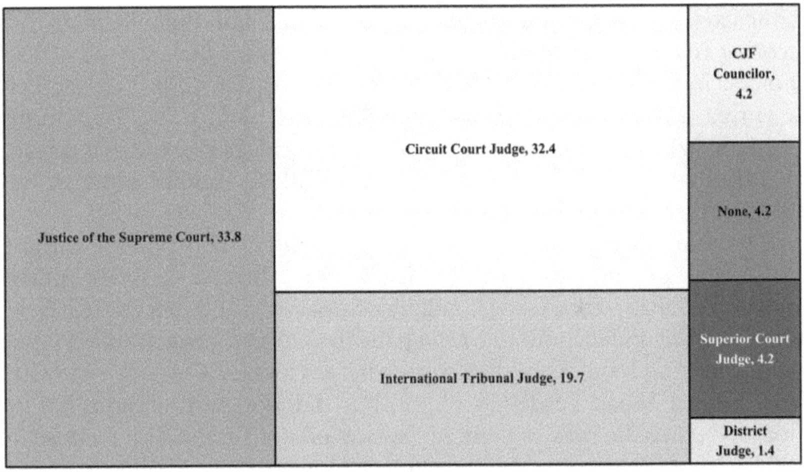

Fig. 4.2 Goals in the judicial career (*Source* Judicial Power Database in Mexico, 2019)

confirm this idea—for example, their strong "commitment" as the main motivation to start working in the judiciary despite the high workload to which they have been subjected throughout their career within the judiciary. Indeed, several studies have shown that the workload within the judiciary is very high: court secretaries and clerks, bailiffs, and judicial officers regularly work more than 12-hour days (Judicial Power Database Field Notes, 2019). During our fieldwork, several judges remarked that the key to ascending to the highest echelons of the judicial career is the possession of qualities such as discipline, perseverance, and a willingness to thrive under pressure. This is perceived with enthusiasm, as the prevailing belief is that the greater the effort, the more assured the reward of promotion becomes.

Lastly, another factor that contributes to shaping the judges' profiles is their admiration for the Supreme Court Justices who serve as sources of inspiration to them. The judicial hierarchy, as well as the nature of the rulings championed by justices, often influences the judges' legal preferences, professional paths, and the way in which courts and judges are organized. Among the justices who served on the Supreme Court in 2018, 52% expressed a stronger affinity, primarily, for then-Justice José Ramón Cossío Díaz. In contrast, 24% identified Justice Margarita Luna

Ramos as their first preference in terms of affinity, with the remaining 12% favoring Justice Jorge Mario Pardo Rebolledo. As for their second affinity choices, 29% of the surveyed judges leaned toward Arturo Zaldívar Lelo de Larrea, 22% favored Minister Pardo Rebolledo, and 17% cited Minister Cossío Díaz. In the third position, 18% of the judges expressed an affinity for Minister Pardo Rebolledo, 16% for Luis María Aguilar Morales, and 15% for Minister Luna Ramos.

The affinities expressed by the surveyed judges also provide insights into their legal culture, as will be discussed in Chapter 6. By examining the professional backgrounds and trajectories of those they admire, we gain a deeper understanding of the path they might want to follow, their legal values and variables that shape them. Cossio Díaz is a renowned jurist with a broad academic career, but did not have a career in the judiciary when he was appointed Justice of the SCJN. From 1990 to 1994, Cossio Díaz served as secretary of study and account to the then-Justice Ulises Schmill Ordoñez and as his coordinator of advisors when he was President of the SCJN. During his academic career, he wrote numerous books and is recognized as a member of the national system of researchers of the National Council of Science and Technology (SCJN, 2016). With Cossio Díaz's arrival at the Supreme Court, he distinguished himself by introducing a new model of advisory team (*ponencia*) (Cortez, 2019). He selected both secretaries with experience in the judicial career, aligning with the practices of most other justices, and lawyers with an academic background and professional litigation experience—an entirely novel approach within the SCJN up to that point. He is recognized as one of the few interpretative and progressive justices to have served on the SCJN since 1994 (Sánchez et al., 2011: 207), a distinction attributed not only to his rulings but also to his legal practice.

On the other hand, Luna Ramos has been a member of the judiciary since 1975, when she began her judicial career. Like many of our respondents, she has climbed most of the steps of the judicial ladder: judicial officer, actuary, project secretary in court, project secretary in collegiate court, member of the Judicial Council, secretary of study and account at the SCJN, district judge, circuit judge, and, finally, Justice of the Supreme Court (SCJN, 2016). Her advisory team (*ponencia*) primarily consisted of secretaries who were members of the judicial career with no external profiles (Cortez, 2019). Luna Ramos' votes in the plenary have been recognized as center-right and as having legalistic tendencies (Sánchez et al., 2011: 207).

Justice Jorge Mario Pardo Rebolledo's professional trajectory is also rooted in his judicial career. With close family ties within the judiciary, from a "young age he played in the hallways of the Supreme Court" (Michel, 2014: 1). He began his career in the judiciary in 1982 and has held various positions, including actuary, court secretary, secretary of study and account, district judge, and circuit magistrate. In 2011, he was appointed as a Justice of the Supreme Court (SCJN, 2016).

Justice Arturo Zaldívar also hails from a background outside the traditional judicial career. Prior to his nomination for this position, he served as an academic and a practicing lawyer (SCJN, 2016). In political terms, his profile as a constitutional judge can be categorized as interpretivist and progressive. He has delivered landmark judgments in defense of human rights, although not all of them have garnered favorable votes in the plenary. In 2019 Zaldívar became the first justice without a judicial career to preside over the SCJN since the reform of 1994. Finally, Minister Luis María Aguilar Morales has had a prolific career in the judiciary, where he has held various positions related not only to the jurisdictional work, but also the management and administration of the judiciary. He embarked on his career in the judiciary in 1968 as a stenographer, subsequently holding positions as a court secretary, secretary of the collegiate court, secretary of study and account at the SCJN, district judge, circuit magistrate, General Secretary of the Presidency, and Chief Clerk of the SCJN. In 2009, he was appointed as a Justice of the Supreme Court and, subsequently, he was elected as its president.

These are the profiles of justices who serve as the most significant sources of inspiration for judges within the PJF. This data allows us to infer that respondents highly regard both academic accomplishments and a career within the judiciary when considering their sources of professional inspiration. There is a trend among judges to mix a traditional and conservative judge profile with another that incorporates novel and progressive aspects. This trend suggests that outsiders to the judiciary are, to some extent, respected and well regarded when they assume jurisdictional roles at the highest level of the Mexican judiciary, particularly those who come from academic and litigation backgrounds. However, this dynamic is not so evident when it comes to positions within the traditional judicial career, such as district judges and circuit magistrates. In these roles, the judges appear to be more closed, and there is evidence suggesting that it is nearly impossible to join the judicial career if one is not already a member of this branch of government through positions like secretaries or bailiffs, among others. The positions such as those of judges and magistrates are open, for the most part, to those who have followed a professional career in the judiciary as judicial officers, bailiffs, or secretaries (see the next chapter), even though the law contemplates that the opposition contests should also be open to the public. Hence, the surveyed judges acknowledge the importance or desirability of a constitutional judge possessing sociopolitical qualities or a background with experience beyond the judiciary. However, they reject this possibility for the most senior and crucial positions within the judicial career, giving precedence to "judicial purity" in the case of district judges and circuit magistrates. In fact, during the survey collection, several judges were concerned that the opposition contests could be open to the public because "someone without jurisdictional experience could become a judge or magistrate" (Judicial Power in Mexico Database, 2019). The federal judiciary appears to be evolving into a closed, insular environment, populated by individuals who have a preference for colleagues with backgrounds within the federal judiciary.

Conclusions

The profiles, sociopolitical origins, and career paths of the judicial elite in Mexico display a significant degree of heterogeneity and diversity. It cannot be affirmed that those who inhabit the palaces of federal justice come from a family with deep roots and a long tradition in the judiciary. Judges have successfully ascended the social hierarchy and now hold positions of immense prestige and influence within state institutions. While their social origins may not be exclusively elite, they have indeed become part of the elite over time. As seen in this chapter, a large proportion of judges come from families with medium–low incomes and mostly with a single provider (the father). Judges do not typically come from prominent political families either. In fact, the judicial elite often asserts its detachment from the world of partisan politics, aligning with its principles and beliefs concerning the separation of politics and the law (see Chapter 6).

Where greater uniformity is observed among judges is in their educational backgrounds and professional paths. Many of them have studied at public, national, and tuition-free universities. This observation can imply two things. First, it suggests that their families may have been limited in their financial capacity and could only afford studies at public institutions, providing insights into their socioeconomic background. Second, it indicates that public universities are often regarded as the most prestigious and recommended for studying law if one aspires to enter the judiciary. It is within these public institutions that connections and relationships are often formed, which can pave the way for opportunities within federal courts. Their education in these universities typically adhered to a traditional educational model, emphasizing memorization as a central aspect of their learning process. However, this approach evolved during their postgraduate studies, where the training they have received has been more focused on the analysis and argumentation of real cases, which contributes to changing legal conceptions and the role of judges in the political system (see Chapter 6). Regarding their professional paths, judges' primary work lies within state institutions, and obtaining a position in the federal judiciary is considered one of the most prestigious achievements. Nearly all of them express high levels of satisfaction with their choice of having become judges in the federal judiciary. Moreover, many aspire to culminate their careers at the pinnacle of the judicial realm, either as a justice in the Supreme Court or in an international court.

Ultimately, the profiles of constitutional judges who serve as the greatest sources of inspiration for them tend to be a blend of individuals from outside the judiciary, possessing strong academic credentials, and those with strictly judicial career backgrounds. In fact, as we will see in Chapter 6, these preferences are also reflected in the types of legal culture that prevail among the judges: a mix of positivism and argumentative constitutionalism. Moreover, the individuals who serve as sources of inspiration for judges offer invaluable insights into the aspirational profiles that they endeavor to cultivate throughout their judicial careers. By examining the qualities and achievements of these esteemed figures, judges gain a clearer understanding of the professional attributes and values they aspire to embody. Consequently, these inspirational figures play a pivotal role in shaping the trajectory and development of judges within the judiciary, guiding them towards a comprehensive and impactful judicial career.

Notes

1. Holding the position of circuit judge is a common response especially among electoral judges, since as mentioned before not all judges of the electoral court of the federal judiciary belong to the judicial career.

2. A smaller proportion of the judges also said they participate and are members of the Mexican Association of Judges and the Mexican Association of Female Judges (for the case of female judges and magistrates).

Bibliography

Aguiar-Aguilar, A., & Torres, I. (2022). Explaining the Sources of Judges' Legal Conceptions in the Mexican Judiciary. *Latin American Law Review, 9*, 117–137.

Ai Camp, R. (2002). *Mexico's Mandarins: Crafting a Power Elite for the Twenty-First Century*. University of California Press.

Alcántara, M. (2014). Some General and Introductory Considerations to the Study of Political Elites in Latin America. *Iberoamericana, 14*(54), 155–159.

ANMJ-PJF. (2022). *About JUFED*. https://jufed.org/.

Arellano, A. (2012). Trajectories, Networks and Recruitment Mechanisms in the Supreme Court of Jalisco. *Sociological Studies of the College of Mexico, 30*(88), 87–118.

Barragán, M. (2015). The Study of Parliamentary Elites in Latin America. Past, Present and Future. *Andean Journal of Political Studies*, *5*(2), 4–30.

Barragán, M., Rivas, C., & Bohigues García, A. (2020). Latin American Parliamentary Elites: How has the Profile of Representation Evolved? *Spanish Journal of Sociology, 29*(3), 613–633.

Best, H., & Cotta, M. (2000). Elite Transformation and Modes of Representation since the Mid-Nineteenth Century: Some Theoretical Considerations. In H. Best & M. Cotta (Eds.), *Parliamentary Representatives in Europe 1848–2000. Legislative recruitments and Careers in Eleven European Countries* (pp. 1–28). Oxford University Press.

Caballero, J. (2006). The Jurisdictional Profile of Federal Judges. *Journal of the Federal Judiciary Institute, 22*, 281–312.

Cortez, J. (2019). Study and Account Secretaries in the Supreme Court of Mexico: An Essential but Forgotten Actor. *Politics and Government, 26*(2), 219–236.

Cuéllar, A. (2008). *The Judges of Tradition. A Case Study*. FCPyS-UNAM.

Dahl, R. (1961). *Who Governs? Democracy and Power in an American City*. Yale University Press.

Donatello, L., & Lorenc, F. (2017). The Rise to the Judicial Elite. A Reconstruction of the Origins and Trajectories of Judges from Biographical Interviews. *Argentine Sociology Journal, 11*(19–20), 6–29.

Fix-Fierro, H. (2020). *The Power of the Judiciary and the Legal Modernization in Contemporary Mexico*. IIJ-UNAM.

Guarnieri, C. (2003). Courts as an Instrument of Horizontal Accountability. In J. M. Maravall and A. Przeworski (Eds.), *Democracy and the Rule of Law* (pp. 223–241). Cambridge: Cambridge University Press.

INEGI. (2020). *Population and Housing Census 2020*.

Judicial Power Database. (2019). Available under request in https://aguiarazul.wordpress.com/contact/

Judicial Power Database Field Notes. (2019). Available under request at https://aguiarazul.wordpress.com/contact/

Judicial Power Database in Mexico. (2019). Available under request in https://aguiarazul.wordpress.com/contact/

Magaloni, A. (2006). Bottlenecks and Windows of Opportunity for Reform and Elite Legal Education in Mexico. In H. Fix-Fierro (Ed.), *From the Government of Lawyers to the Empire of Laws. Socio-Legal Studies on Education and Legal Profession in Contemporary Mexico* (pp. 61–91). IIJ-UNAM.

Magaloni, B. (2003). Authoritarianism, Democracy and the Supreme Court: Horizontal Exchange and the Rule of Law in Mexico. In S. Mainwaring & C. Welna (Eds.), *Democratic Accountability in Latin America* (pp. 266–306). Oxford University Press.

Michel, E. (2014, October 31). Pardo Rebolledo, Dreamed of Being a Minister Since he was a Child. *El Universal*.

Montaño, M. (2017). Introduction. In F. Patrón and M. Montaño (Eds.), *Local Parliamentary Elites in Mexico: Attitudes and Performance* (pp. 13–24). Tirant Lo Blanch.

PJF Biographical Files Database. (2022). Available under request in https://aguiarazul.wordpress.com/contact/

Ríos-Figueroa, J. (2018, August 27). The Meritocratic Deficit. Nepotism and family Networks in the Federal Judicial Power. *Nexos*.

Sadek, M. (2006). *Magistrates: An Image in Motion*. Editora FGV.

Sadek, M. (2010). The Judiciary Crisis Seen by Judges: Results of a quantitative research. In M. Sadek (Ed.), *An Introduction to the Study of Justice* (pp. 17–31). Centro Edelstein of Social Research.

Sánchez, A., Magaloni, B., & Magar, E. (2011). Legalist vs. Interpretativist: The Supreme Court and the Democratic Transition in Mexico. In G. Helmke and J. Ríos-Figueroa (Eds.), *Courts in Latin America* (pp. 187–218). Cambridge University Press.

SCJN. (2016). *Profiles of the Ministers of the Supreme Court of Justice of the Nation. 1917–2016*. SCJN.

Werneck, L., Rezende, M., Cunha, M., & Baumann, M. (1997). *Body and Soul of the Brazilian Magistracy*. Revan.

CHAPTER 5

The Internal Dynamics of the Judiciary: Recruitment and Judicial Career

Abstract This chapter is dedicated to exploring judges' recruitment and judicial career, and follows up on their social origins and professional trajectory. It presents data on the entry paths into the federal judiciary, the career trajectories within it, and the perceptions regarding the functioning of the judicial career and the factors that matter for promotion. As a starting point, it examines the different models of judicial governance that have operated or are currently operating in judicial systems, including the patronage model, the recognition model, and the professional career service model. To different extents, these models continue to be part of the recruitment logic within the Mexican judiciary.

Keywords Judicial career · Judicial recruitment · Judicial promotions · Judicial governance model

The house of justice should be staffed by professionals. This premise can be traced back to the idea of the "artificial reason" originally proposed by Sir Edward Coke (1986), who in the seventeenth century pointed out that judges should be only responsible for rendering verdicts due to their competence, experience, in-depth understanding of legal procedures, and extensive knowledge of the law—they are thoroughly prepared for this

A. A. Aguiar Aguilar, *Legal Culture, Sociopolitical Origins and Professional Careers of Judges in Mexico*,
https://doi.org/10.1007/978-3-031-52909-2_5

role. With this idea, Coke sought to limit the power of the King to decide cases, as these cannot be decided from the "natural reason" that kings possess, but from the intelligence and specialized training, "the artificial reason," that judges achieved through the study and practice of law. By doing this, the then president of the English Court laid the foundations not only of judicial independence, but particularly what we now recognize as the professionalization and establishment of a judicial career—a system where judges possess specialized skills, undergo continuous training, and follow a merit-based trajectory.

Judicial professionalization is a key issue to fulfill the mandate and promise of justice. However, the judiciary has not consistently been staffed by individuals possessing the requisite capacities, experience, and legal skills to fulfill the promise of the house of justice. Before the transition to democracy, for example, the judiciaries of several Latin American countries were part of a well-articulated clientelistic system: a selection process based on patronage and clientelistic practices prevailed. Members of the elite from the ruling political party's inner circle held positions in various tiers of the judiciary, ranging from lower-level positions to the intermediate and upper echelons, which called into question the quality and integrity of justice and judicial institutions.

In Mexico, judges of the federal judiciary had managed to install a family network at different levels of the institution (Borrego, 2017; Ríos-Figueroa, 2018). However, as Coke pointed out, judges should be independent and professional, as they are called upon to issue rulings that resolve conflicts between powers and seek to protect the rights of citizens. Judicial reforms aimed to replace cronyism with a merit-based system for the intermediate levels of the federal judiciary and implemented a recognition or appointment system for the highest positions in the Supreme Court. Regarding the introduction of a professional career system based on merit, these reforms followed the experience of continental European judiciaries and created judicial councils to improve the internal governance of the judiciary and increase judicial independence. These bureaucratic models of judicial governance are responsible for managing the various aspects of the judicial career, including the selection, training, appointment, promotion, and disciplinary actions related to judges. They also oversee the implementation of transparency and judicial accountability mechanisms. Judicial councils are a foundation upon which both external and internal independence of judges is built. On the one hand, they protect judges from interference from other state powers and, on the other hand, they prevent the career of judges from depending on superior judges and not on merits, skills, and qualifications.

Despite the judicial reform of 1994 in Mexico, which granted a new organization, institutional structure, and a professional career to the federal judiciary, the process of becoming a judge still relies on the personal network that the candidate has within the judiciary. In fact, a recent report indicates that there is a "meritocratic deficit" in the judiciary: "51% of judges have at least one relative working in the federal judiciary" (Ríos-Figueroa, 2018: 7). This does not mean that the judicial career system in the federal judiciary does not work at all. Instead, we can argue that several factors contribute to the suboptimal performance of this system, promoting the formation of a closed-knit judicial circle that hinders the much-needed diversification of profiles within the judiciary.

How are judges recruited? What matters for their ratification and promotion? How does the judicial career work? What motivations and incentives drove judges to obtain a position in the judiciary? By answering these questions, this chapter expands on previous research dedicated to understanding the internal dynamics of the judiciary, in particular, the professional trajectory and judicial career followed by judges (Garoupa & Ginsburg, 2011; Georgakopoulos, 2000; Guarnieri, 2004; Pozas-Loyo & Ríos-Figueroa, 2018). This chapter is divided into four sections. The second section offers a brief review of the literature on judicial governance, namely, the different models in which the judiciary can be organized and governed internally. Here special attention is paid to the so-called professional judicial career system. Using the data collected in the survey with federal judges, the third section presents the results that allow us to understand how candidates go from assistants to clerk secretaries, and ultimately to judges and magistrates. The chapter closes with a reflection on the judicial professionalization of judges in Mexico.

Models of Recruitment and Judicial Governance

The professional profile of judicial actors plays a key role in judicial behavior and the administration of justice. Judicial behavior largely depends on the individual preferences of judges, which are determined by the institutional framework of the judiciary, the legal framework, their ideas, or their merits and professional trajectory, to name some important explanatory variables. We can expect different types of judicial decisions depending on how, for example, the professional trajectory of judges is structured—that is, how a judge is recruited, selected, trained, ratified, dismissed or promoted to higher ranks.

Contemporary political systems have experienced at least three different models of judicial governance: patronage, meritocratic, and recognition. The first of these has been prevalent in autocratic governments or politically underdeveloped systems. Clientelist or patronage systems are characterized by the logic of exchange, in which the patron offers something (for example, positions in public office) to the client in exchange for support and loyalty. Under this system, executives or political parties in power fills the judiciary with candidates loyal to their political project. Judges respond to the will of the executive and leave their court seat when the executive decides, so their career is more political than judicial. This model finds a compelling illustration in the case of Mexico during the era of electoral authoritarianism under the PRI which lasted until the judicial reform of 1994. During this period, judges, including those on the Supreme Court, were known to vacate their positions to assume roles as state secretaries, governors, or senators when requested by the president (Magaloni, 2003).

The legal systems of representative democracies developed two models of judicial governance: the "recognition system" and the "career system" (Garoupa & Ginsburg, 2011; Georgakopoulos, 2000). The "recognition" judicial governance model is based on appointments of recognized legal professionals who have previously built distinguished careers as scholars or practicing jurists. These appointments are usually made by the executive and/or the legislature and are more widespread in countries with legal systems of *common law,* such as the United States. Judges do not necessarily pursue a career path within the judiciary, meaning they are not obligated to ascend through a specific hierarchy to attain the highest positions. The career judicial system is a merit system that recruits its members with no more professional competencies than a law degree, to then professionalize them along a judicial bureaucratic path. The recruitment, appointment, training, promotion, dismissal, and evaluation is carried out through a model of judicial governance known as the judicial council and is predominant in *civil law* legal systems. Garoupa and Ginsburg point out that these models of judicial organization do not prevail in a pure form in any country, and most jurisdictions have hybrid systems, which combine aspects of both recognition and merit-based judicial career systems (Garoupa & Ginsburg, 2011: 418–419). In some Latin American countries judges in the intermediate and lower courts tend to formally follow a judicial career, while the higher ranks (justices of the Supreme Court or of specialized constitutional courts) are appointed by the executive and the legislature from a group of career judges or candidates without a judicial career, but with recognized trajectories in the free practice of law.

Some scholars argue that a merit-based judicial career system lays the foundations for attaining judges with heightened levels of professionalization, effectively shielding the judiciary from political interferences (Di Federico, 2005; Phillips, 2009). Unlike recognition systems, where politics has a clear influence on who becomes a judge, the European-continental legal tradition elaborated on and adopted bureaucratic models of judicial governance to manage the process of selection, training, promotion, and evaluation of lower-ranking judges (Guarnieri, 2008; Piana, 2010). This resulted in the consolidation of strong, independent judiciaries that set clear limits to the other two powers, particularly during pivotal political junctures, such as instances of political corruption. This is the case of *mani pulite* in Italy, where both the judiciary and the prosecutors managed to carry out judicial processes that profoundly transformed the Italian political system. However, the idea that the judicial career system produces these effects is not shared by everyone. Some scholars, especially from countries where recruitment is done through the recognition system or by elections, question the advantages that the meritocratic judicial career system could bring, especially when it comes to the expectation that this model produces in terms of judicial independence, accountability, the appropriate role of the courts, or the behavior of judges (Owens et al., 2015; Taylor, 2009). Scholars postulate that even if a merit system is adopted to fill a position, "politics will always play a role in the selection of judges" (Taylor, 2009: 101). However, the merit-based judicial career system in justice institutions has value not only because it can restrict political influence more effectively in the selection process but, also because it mandates judges to undergo training, gain practical experience, and excel in their roles as judges if they aspire to ascend to higher positions. This is particularly important in countries with recent authoritarian pasts, where the clientelistic model of judicial recruitment was the basis on which judges developed their careers.

When analyzing the outcomes of merit-based judicial career system, comparative judicial politics has studied the role played by judicial councils or commissions (Di Federico, 2005; Garoupa et al., 2012; Garoupa &

Ginsburg, 2008; Guarnieri, 2008). The experiences of several countries, including France, Italy, Germany, Spain, and Brazil, demonstrate that judicial councils serve as custodians of officials' professional profiles and oversee the performance of the institution. These models of judicial governance are involved in the careful recruitment, evaluation, promotion, relocation, and dismissal of judges. Their composition varies by country, but most include members of the judiciary elected by their peers and external members (experienced lawyers or law scholars) appointed by the executive and legislative branches (Guarnieri, 2004). Judicial council members are appointed to serve for a specific period and, in some countries, can be ratified for a second term. Experience has shown that councils with a larger number of members belonging to the judiciary make the institution more independent from external influences (Guarnieri, 2011), but, on some occasions, also less *accountable*.

A central role of judicial councils is to regulate and manage the judicial career, encompassing the professionalization, discipline, and promotion of the professional growth of judges in various positions of the judicial hierarchy based on their performance. Professionalization implies the existence of a merit-based judicial career system that guides the career of officials within judicial institutions. In countries such as France, Germany, and Italy, judicial councils manage the careers of judges and prosecutors with the aim not only of shielding them from political influences, but especially of professionalizing them and making them accountable: judges and prosecutors undergo several trainings and evaluations before and after obtaining their appointment (Guarnieri, 2004) and, once in the position, they follow the process of supervision and evaluation of their jurisdictional work to ascend in rank.

Recruitment in a merit-based judicial career system is carried out in the early stages of candidates' careers, usually after obtaining their law degree. Access to the judiciary is obtained after passing exams (written and oral) in an open and public competition with limited vacancies. The selected candidates are appointed as judicial assistants and begin a period of on-the-job training in which they familiarize themselves with the different areas of law (criminal, labor, family, commercial, etc.). After this period, and sometimes following a second exam as is the case in Germany, they are appointed to subordinate positions (typically trial room secretaries), from which they will make their career to the highest ranks available in the judiciary (Georgakopoulos, 2000; Guarnieri, 2004). In some cases such as in France, pre- and post-appointment training is assigned to judicial schools, an entity that manages academic accreditation and suitability for the position of career judges by organizing seminars, specializations, and postgraduate programs. Evaluations, promotions, relocations, and dismissals are managed and evaluated by the judicial council considering the experience, performance, behavior, seniority, and/or training of the judges. The salary of judges is fixed and increases as they reach the highest positions in the judiciary or, in some cases, as in Italy or Germany, with seniority (Guarnieri, 2004).

Recruitment systems rooted in clientelistic policies, recognition, or merit yield varying effects on the composition of judges within the judiciary, their independence from other actors, and the judgments they render. For the first model (the clientelistic one), we could expect judges where "natural reason" predominates over "artificial reason," as it is the political will of the person in power that fills the house of justice. For the recognition model, we can expect judges experienced in law and who will not hide their political preferences when passing sentences. Ultimately, the merit-based judicial career system aspires to produce judges whose entry into and continued presence within the judiciary are contingent upon their technical-legal competence, thereby prioritizing "artificial reason" over "natural reason" and fostering the emergence of more independent and professional judges.

Pathways to Becoming a Judge in the Federal Judiciary

During the era of authoritarian governments in Mexico, presidents came and left power with their own courts: the Mexican presidents from 1934 to 1994 changed on average more than 50% of the justices of the Supreme Court during their administrations (Magaloni, 2003: 288). Becoming a justice of the Supreme Court in Mexico often required one to have a close association with the president or demonstrating loyalty to the party. This external dependence made it evident that the judiciary was subordinated, as one might expect. But the judiciary goes beyond the Supreme Court. In the lower ranks of the federal judiciary, we could not talk about professionalization, meritocracy, or judicial careers as we saw in the previous section. A clientelist model persisted because, from 1917, Supreme Court justices informally assumed the authority to appoint judges and magistrates for the district and circuit courts. Neither the

Constitution nor secondary law regulating the judiciary stipulated the procedure for appointing them. Thus, justices eventually developed an informal institution, a "Gentlemen's Pact," meaning a practice in which the justices took turns to fill vacancies and then managed the career of their own judges (Pozas-Loyo & Ríos-Figueroa, 2018: 650). The "Gentlemen's Pact" consolidated a career for the judges based on a clientelistic system, in which the justices had the power to create subnational courts—from administrative and technical positions to judgeships—and populate them with their loyalists (friends or even relatives). In addition, justices performed the roles of promotion, supervision, and protection of their appointees throughout their career within the judiciary (Carpizo, 2001).

The reform of the federal judiciary in 1994 sought to change this pattern by formally establishing a hybrid system of judicial government that combines a merit-based judicial career system for judges in circuit and district courts, and a recognition model for the justices of the Supreme Court and the electoral magistrates in the Electoral Court. A pivotal aspect of the meritocratic model of the judicial career was the establishment of the Federal Judicial Council, which took on the responsibilities that were formerly solely within the purview of the Supreme Court justices, including recruitment, selection, promotion, and evaluation of, as well as disciplinary actions for, judges throughout their careers. In essence, it spearheaded the professionalization of judges within the judicial career.

Currently, access to the federal judiciary in Mexico varies according to positions and ranks, and, due to the reforms but also despite them, we can verify the existence of: a) the recognition model; b) the meritocratic model; and c) the clientelistic model. The judges of the Electoral Courts are appointed through a recognition system using a list prepared by the Supreme Court and voted in by two-thirds of the Senate. Candidates on this list may include individuals who are career judges, as well as candidates without prior judicial experience, but who possess a legal background acknowledged by the political group that select them in the Senate. The positions of the judges of the Electoral Courts are then more prone to political influences in the nomination process. This has resulted in a kind of stigma for electoral judges within the federal judiciary. For instance, in the period when the surveys were conducted, an electoral tribunal magistrate contended that district and circuit judges tend to marginalize them. They were not convinced that electoral magistrates were integral to the judiciary, primarily because many of them had not undergone the entrance and selection exams that formally induct individuals into the judiciary. In fact, some circuit magistrates and district judges pointed out that the electoral judges were "of course" part of the judiciary, but they were "different" in the sense that they were "more political" and were not suited to a judicial career (Judicial Power Database in Mexico, 2019). It is important to note that this opinion does not extend to the justices of the Supreme Court. In other words, constitutional judges enjoy widespread recognition and legitimacy among career judges, even though, as we have observed, they are also appointed through a recognition system that considers candidates with or without a judicial career.

The majority of the judges who were surveyed entered the judiciary when judicial career was formally composed of the following positions[1]: circuit judge (collegiate), district judge, secretary and sub-secretary of the Supreme Court and the Electoral Court, secretary of the circuit court, secretary of the district court, and assistant and secretary of the appeal courts (Article 110 Ley Orgánica del Poder Judicial de la Federación, 2019). However, these positions differed in the way in which each one was achieved and managed—that is, not all positions in judicial careers followed the logic and structure of a meritocratic career system (as described in the previous section). For the position of district judge and circuit magistrate, the judicial council organizes an exam (written and oral) with legal and academic content, which could be open or closed to members of the judiciary. From 1995 to 2016, the majority of opposition exams (87%) were closed—that is, only candidates who already worked in the judiciary could apply (Ríos-Figueroa, 2018). During fieldwork, a district judge mentioned that closed calls were the Achilles' heel of the judicial career in Mexico, as it prevented non-judicial profiles from being considered for vacancies in district and circuits courts, but also because the calls issued by the judicial council naturally tended to favor people who already worked in the judiciary—that is, they restricted participation to those applicants with experience as, for example, district and circuit court secretaries (Judicial Power Database in Mexico, 2019). As will be analyzed below, in order to secure the position of court secretary, candidates were not required to undergo a stringent examination or competency assessment process.

For positions at the lower levels of the judicial career, such as secretaries, clerks, and sub-secretaries in various district, circuit, and Electoral

Courts, applicants were only required to take an aptitude test (Article 111 LOPJF, 2019), meaning a non-competitive or non-rigorous exam. The judicial council was not mandated to publicly announce open competitions to fill vacancies in the lower positions of the judicial career, but only to apply an aptitude test that was subsequently evaluated by the judge or magistrate who had a vacancy. Consequently, the selection and appointment of court secretaries and clerks fell on the judge or magistrate whose court had the vacancy (Article 115 LOPJF, 2019). This posed a challenge because, for 33.8% of the judges in the sample, their first role within the judiciary was as a court secretary (Fig. 5.1). This contrasts with the judicial career model observed in some countries such as Italy or France, where meticulous recruitment begins at the lowest levels of the judicial hierarchy.

The lowest-ranking career position within the judiciary is that of clerk and 17% of the judges in the sample achieved it as their first position in the PJF (Fig. 5.1). No opposition exam was required to obtain the position of clerk and, to be considered, candidates only had to present an aptitude test to the judicial council. As with court secretaries, the appointment was in the hands of the district and circuit judges, who freely chose the candidate to fill the vacancy from a list provided by the judicial council (Article 115 LOPJF, 2019). Generally, judges selected the candidate to occupy the position from among their own judicial assistants or those from other courts within the federal judiciary. It was rare for judges to appoint candidates who were not previously employees in the judiciary (Caballero, 2006: 288).

Finally, there were also "trusted" positions when the judges surveyed here entered the judiciary. In these types of positions, judges assign candidates to a vacancy because they know them or have recommendations from other judges. In this category falls the position of judicial officer (or administrative officer), whose main task is to assist the secretary. The role of judicial officer was the second most-held "first position" among the judges surveyed when they initially joined the judiciary, with 32% of the judges in the collected sample occupying this position (Fig. 5.1). To fill the judicial-administrative officer vacancies, no open or closed competitions are organized: the judge is legally empowered to freely appoint trust positions in his jurisdiction. Generally, the candidates for the position of judicial-administrative officer are law interns, students, or relatives recommended by the judges.

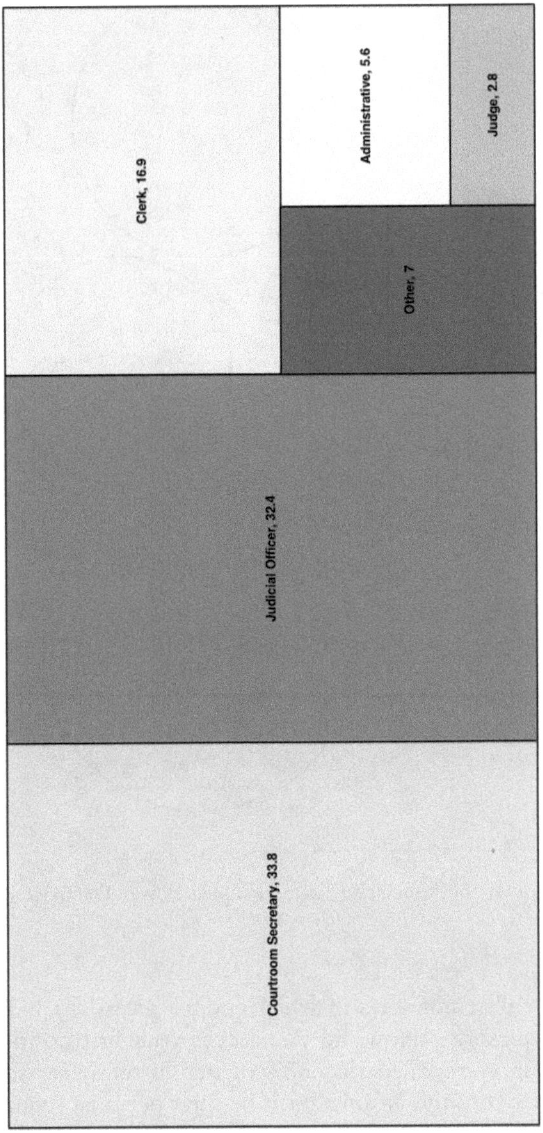

Fig. 5.1 First position in the judiciary (*Source* Judicial Power Database in Mexico, 2019)

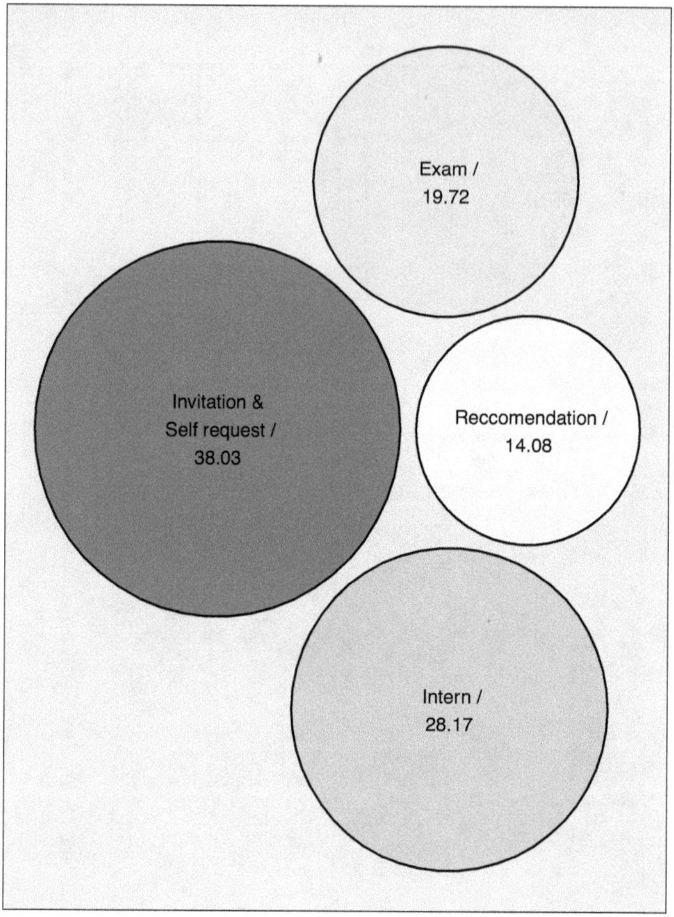

Fig. 5.2 The door of the judiciary (*Source* Judicial Power Database in Mexico, 2019)

There are four different ways in which judges access the judiciary. In response to the question "How did you secure your first position in the judiciary?" the survey revealed that 38% of the currently serving judges stated it was either through an invitation or their personal request to the head of the court. Another 28% mentioned that they began as interns (usually unpaid students gaining experience), and 14% indicated that a recommendation had facilitated their entry into the judiciary. Only 20% claimed to have participated in some form of competition (Fig. 5.2), with a significant number of these judges being those assigned to the Electoral Court. As mentioned earlier, appointments of electoral judges are made through the recognition system, with the Supreme Court selecting a list of candidates, which is then forwarded to the Senate for the final selection and nomination for the position (Fig. 5.2)[2]. This situation reflects a system that leans more toward clientelism rather than meritocracy, as entry was not contingent on rigorous and competitive examinations, but rather on luck, personal connections, or social status for those seeking to build their careers within the federal judiciary. This is further supported by some of the motivations cited by judges for entering the judiciary.

Judges have various motivations for joining the federal judiciary. The surveyed judges saw it as an attractive and prestigious institution in which to make their careers, especially compared to other public institutions like state judiciaries, public defenders or prosecutor's offices. The federal judiciary is the most accredited institution for those who as lawyers want to venture into the institutions of the justice sector. Being part of the federal judiciary is considered by the judges as more rewarding professionally, socially, and materially than other options they might have as legal professionals in the public sector. Additionally, the judges were convinced that working in the judiciary could make a difference in their lives and those of others. When we asked the judges about the reasons why they joined the federal judiciary, the most frequently mentioned words in their responses were as follows:

a. "Commitment": driven by a personal commitment to contribute to the administration of justice and to be a part of a reputable institution like the Mexican Federal Judiciary.
b. "Recommendation": because someone vouched for them and assisted in securing their employment.
c. "Professor": because a professor extended an invitation to them to join.
d. "Justice": to improve justice in the country.
e. "Judge": because a judge extended an invitation to them to join.
f. "Invitation": due to the invitation they received from a relative, professor, judge, or friend.
g. "Vocation": because they felt a calling to become a judge.

h. "Career": because attracted by the prospect of building and the associated prestige.
i. "Brother": because they had a brother in the federal judiciary.

Thus, the motivations for judges to enter the federal judiciary can be grouped into two categories: one that is close to a meritocratic model (career, justice, vocation, and commitment) and another that is closer to a clientelistic model (recommendation, brother, professor, and judge). The meritocratic model encompasses motivations rooted in principles of career advancement, dedication to justice, a sense of vocation, and a commitment to upholding the rule of law. Judges who align with this model are driven by a desire to contribute to the legal system's integrity and effectiveness. Conversely, the clientelistic model is characterized by motivations influenced by personal connections, recommendations, familial ties, and patronage networks. Judges who subscribe to this model entered the judiciary through informal channels, such as recommendations from influential individuals like family members, professors, or existing judges. By categorizing judges' motivations along these two distinct paradigms, we gain a nuanced understanding of the diverse factors shaping the composition of the federal judiciary. Moreover, recognizing the interplay between meritocratic and clientelistic influences sheds light on the complexities inherent in judicial recruitment processes and underscores the importance of promoting transparency, accountability, and merit-based selection criteria within the judiciary.

Paths and Dynamics of the Judicial Career

Once a candidate secured a position in the federal judiciary, their path to the higher rungs of the judiciary was more assured compared to any other external candidate—for example, applicants coming from public defender's offices, prosecution services, or state-level judicial powers. However, to become a judge, both professional and political obstacles must be overcome. On the one hand, candidates for a district or circuit court have to work overtime for many years without receiving any payment for this. One of the surveyed judges pointed out that in federal courts "there is no such thing as a work schedule" (Judicial Power Database in Mexico, 2019), but there are duties to fulfill, so employees work during the night or take their work home to cope with the workload and meet deadlines (Ferreyra, 2018). More than 80% of judges strongly agree or agree with the idea that the workload in the judiciary is excessive, and more than 60% of them agree or strongly agree with the fact that more positions are needed in the circuits where they are currently working. Given the excessive workload, about 90% of the judges usually continue their work at home. In fact, about 60% of the judges in the courts acknowledge that the excessive workload hampers their ability to craft well-considered decisions (Graph 5.1).

On the other hand, other barriers (political or jurisdictional) also have to be overcome to become judges and magistrates of the federal judiciary. Graph 5.2 shows the opinions and experiences of the judges in relation to the selection, ratification and promotion process to occupy the position of district and circuit judge. They almost unanimously agree (94%) that to become a judge (district or circuit), the opposition contest is decisive (*ExamDecisive* in Graph 5.2)—that is, they have to take an exam with legal and academic content, write a sentence of a simulated case, and pass an oral exam. Only 6% of the judges have a neutral opinion and would be willing to accept that, in some instances, alternative mechanisms are employed to secure a position in the federal judiciary. These may include garnering the support of a renowned and well-connected judge or magistrate in order to appeal to the Supreme Court against a Judicial Council's decision regarding an applicant's qualification.

When the judges were asked if "only the best profiles access the judicial career" (BestProf in Graph 5.2), 66% agreed or strongly agreed with this idea, and 34% disagreed or strongly disagreed. The judges here were split in their responses in terms of letting us know that not only the best-qualified profiles access the federal judiciary: there are occasions when applicants without the best legal, academic, or professional qualifications have obtained the position of district or circuit judge. In fact, politics plays a role in the ratification of the judges, since 39% of them agreed or strongly agreed with the idea that "judges with political connections have greater opportunities to be ratified in their positions" (PolRatif in Graph 5.2), while 61% disagreed or strongly disagreed with this statement. In any case, the divided responses observed among judges indicate that politics plays a role and judges must take care of their political relationships within the judiciary.

In the same vein, judges believe that their promotion (moving up the ladder) in the judicial career depends on merit and experience, but also on political connections (see Graph 5.2). On the one hand, 79% of them agreed or strongly agreed with the statement that "judges with more

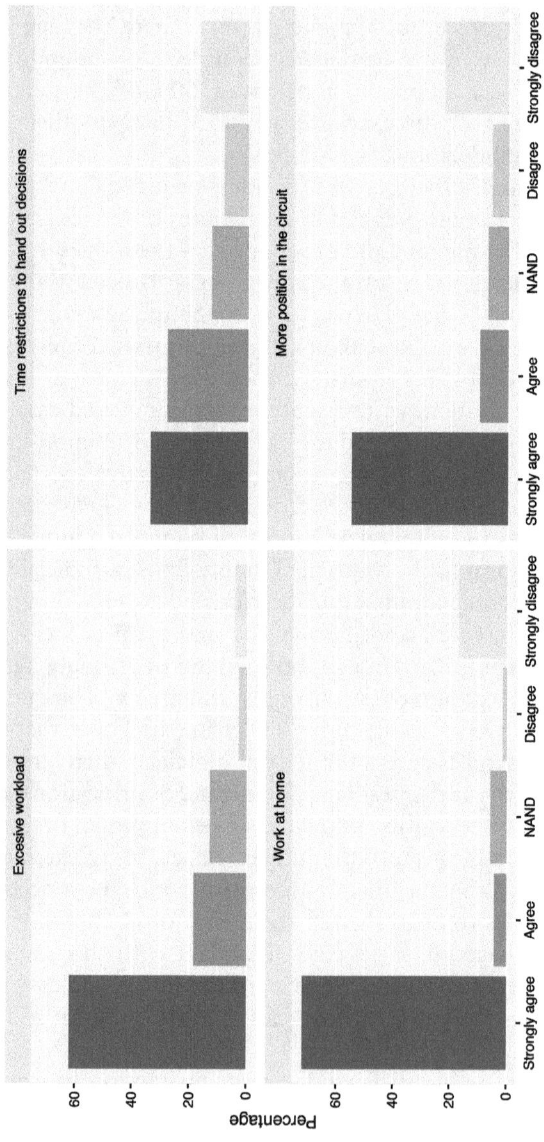

Graph 5.1 Internal dynamics in the judiciary (*Source* Judicial Power Database in Mexico, 2019)

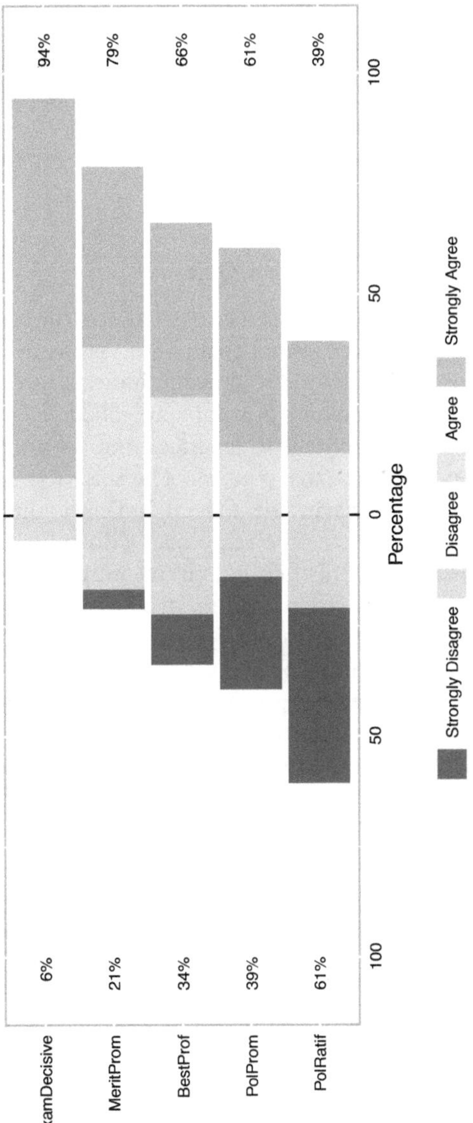

Graph 5.2 Selection, ratification and judicial promotion (*Source* Judicial Power Database in Mexico, 2019)

experience and training have greater opportunities to ascend to higher positions" (MeritProm in Graph 5.2). On the other hand, when asked their opinion on whether "judges with political connections have greater opportunities to be promoted to higher positions" (PolProm in Graph 5.2) 61% agreed or strongly agreed. Therefore, in addition to training, experience, good behavior, and performance, judges needed to develop political relationships that could support their path to the highest ranks in the Mexican federal judiciary.

Conclusions

Mexico has consolidated a judicial career system for the selection and promotion of judges, but it faces several challenges. As has been observed, the most notable complication of the current judicial career is related to the way in which lower-ranking positions are filled, as it allows the reproduction of nepotism, clientelistic practices and closes the door of the judiciary to competitive external profiles. The selection and appointment of lower-ranking officials in the federal judiciary through exams that are considered to "lack academic relevance" (Borrego, 2017: 187), along with the involvement of district and circuit judges in the selection and appointment process, undermine the meritocratic principles and the effectiveness of the judicial career in Mexico. This was possible not only due to institutional design, but also to the configuration of the Judicial Council. Judges control this judicial governance body (composed of seven members, four of whom are selected from among members of the federal judiciary) and decide how competitions are organized: whether they are open or closed, who can participate, and what type of exam should be applied.

Additionally, through legislation representatives have bestowed significant authority upon district and circuit judges to hire lower-ranking personnel within their courts' jurisdiction without the requirement of competitive exams. This legislation has enabled the manipulation of the judicial career by judges, as attaining high-ranking positions in the judiciary is typically only achievable when the candidate is already within the system. Through the law, district and circuit judges have gained authority that was previously held by Supreme Court justices, leading to the perpetuation of a clientelistic system. This system continues to be rooted in the establishment of a judge's professional career through a sociolegal support network, wherein candidates for judicial positions are promoted within their own court or through the assistance of a fellow judge. Candidates for a position need to relate to, meet with, interact with, associate with, and be loyal to practicing judges in order to be accepted as part of the judicial family. The judicial career went from the "Gentlemen's Pact" to one in which district and circuit judges have autonomy over their own jurisdictions.

Thus, political relationships and sociolegal networks play a role in the judicial career path. This is not surprising considering the problems pointed out earlier with regard to the dominant role that judges play in the appointment of lower-ranking career positions (secretaries, bailiffs, and judicial-administrative officers) and the lack of rigor in the selection process.

Consequently, despite the judicial reform that introduced a merit-based judicial career system, becoming a judge does not depend solely on the experience and qualifications of the candidates. In some cases, applicants must be part of at least one sociolegal network that can provide the political support necessary to gain access to and navigate the complexities of the judicial career path. Thus, we can also affirm that the judicial career path is determined not only by how capable a judge is, but also by who they know, who they associate with, who they relate to, or, as a retired justice put it when analyzing the judicial career, who mentors you to have a successful career in the federal judiciary (Cossío, 1996).

Notes

1. Holding the position of circuit judge is a common response especially among electoral judges, as mentioned before not all judges of the Electoral Court of the federal judiciary belong to the judicial career.
2. A smaller proportion of the judges also said they participate and are members of the Mexican Association of Judges and the Mexican Association of Female Judges (for the case of female judges and magistrates).

Bibliography

Borrego, F. (2017). Study on Family and Client Networks in the Federal Judiciary Council. *Mexican Journal of Justice, 29–30*, 159–191.

Caballero, J. (2006). The Jurisdictional Profile of Federal Judges. *Journal of the Federal Judiciary Institute, 22*, 281–312.
Carpizo, J. (2001). Twenty-two Years of Mexican Presidentialism: 1978–2000. A Recapitulation. *Mexican Bulletin of Comparative Law, 24*(100), 71–99.
Coke, Sir Edward. (1986). *Institutes of the Laws of England I*. J.H. Thomas Ed.
Cossío, J. R. (1996). *Notebooks for Judicial Reform: Federal Jurisdiction and Judicial Career in Mexico*. IIJ-UNAM.
Di Federico, G. (2005). *Recruitment, Professional Evaluation and Career of Judges and Prosecutors in Europe: Austria, France, Germany, Italy, the Netherlands and Spain*. Lo Scarabeo.
Ferreyra, G. (2018). Unpacking the Mexican Federal Judiciary: An Inner Look at the Ethos of the Judicial Branch. *Mexican Law Review, 11*(1), 57–83.
Garoupa, N., & Ginsburg, T. (2008). Guarding the Guardians: Judicial Councils and Judicial Independence. *The American Journal of Comparative Law*, 57(1), 103–134.
Garoupa, N., & Ginsburg, T. (2011). Hybrid Judicial Career Structures: Reputation versus Legal Tradition. *Journal of Legal Analysis, 3*(2), 411–448.
Garoupa, N., Gili, M., & Gómez-Pomar, F. (2012). Political Influence and Career Judges: An Empirical Analysis of Administrative Review by the Spanish Supreme Court. *Journal of Empirical Legal Studies, 9*(4), 795–826.
Georgakopoulos, N. (2000). Discretion in the Career and Recognition Judiciary. *Chicago Law School Roundtable, 7*(1), 205–225.
Guarnieri, C. (2004). Appointment and Career of Judges in Continental Europe: The Rise of Judicial Self-Government. *Legal Studies, 24*(1–2), 169–187.
Guarnieri, C. (2008). Magistrates in Europe: Independence, Professionalism, Responsibility: The Italian Case. *Studi Urbinati, A - Juridical, Political and Economic Sciences, 59*(2), 255–264.
Guarnieri, C. (2011). *Berlusconi on Trial: Some Lessons for Judicial Accountability*. The Foundation for Law, Justice and Society.
Judicial Power Database in Mexico, (2019). Available under request at https://aguiarazul.wordpress.com/contact
Magaloni, B. (2003). Authoritarianism, Democracy and the Supreme Court: Horizontal Exchange and the Rule of Law in Mexico. In S. Mainwaring & C. Welna (Eds.), *Democratic Accountability in Latin America* (pp. 266–306). Oxford University Press.
Owens, R., Tahk, A., Wohlfarth, P., & Bryan, A. (2015). Nominating Commissions, Judicial Retention, and Forward-Looking Behavior on State Supreme Courts: An Empirical Examination of Selection and Retention Methods. *State Politics & Policy Quarterly, 15*(2), 211–238.
Phillips, T. (2009). The Merits of Merit Selection. *Harvard Journal of Law & Public Policy, 32*(1), 67–96.

Piana, D. (2010). *Judicial Accountabilities in New Europe. From Rule of Law to Quality of Justice*. Routledge.

Pozas-Loyo, A., & Ríos-Figueroa, J. (2018). Anatomy of an Informal Institution: The 'Gentlemen's Pact' and Judicial Selection in Mexico, 1917–1994. *International Political Science Review, 39*(5), 647–661.

Ríos-Figueroa, J. (2018, August 27). The Meritocratic Deficit. Nepotism and Family Networks in the Federal Judicial Power. *Nexos*.

Taylor, C. (2009). Merit Selection: Choosing Judges Based on Their Politics under the Veil of a Disarming Name. *Harvard Journal of Law & Public Policy, 32*(1), 97–101.

CHAPTER 6

The Legal Culture of the Judicial Elites in Mexico

Abstract This chapter addresses the central task of describing the types of legal culture that currently prevail in the Mexican federal judiciary. The findings demonstrate that there is not a single type of legal culture among judges, nor is it predominantly formalist-positivist. In Mexico, there are judges who hold a constitutionalist-argumentative legal culture, willing to make interpretations to create policies from the bench. However, we can also confirm the presence of a positivist legal culture among them in which deference to enacted law persist. Considering these arguments, judges' opinions regarding rights and freedoms such as abortion, drugs, and same-sex marriage are also analyzed.

Keywords Legal culture · Positivism · Constitutionalism · Argumentativism · Legal formalism · Judges' opinions

---

Some parts of this chapter were previously published in the following articles. Aguiar-Aguilar Azul. A. 2022. Understanding the Judiciary from the Inside. The Legal Culture of Judges in Mexico. *Justice System Journal, 43*(4), 576–592. https://doi.org/10.1080/0098261X.2022.2123288; and Aguiar-Aguilar Azul A. and Ilsse Torres Ortega, Explaining the sources of judges' legal conceptions in the Mexican judiciary. *Latin American Law Review, 1*(9), 117–137. https://doi.org/10.29263/lar09.2022.07

A. A. Aguiar Aguilar, *Legal Culture, Sociopolitical Origins and Professional Careers of Judges in Mexico*,
https://doi.org/10.1007/978-3-031-52909-2_6

In most Latin American democracies, judges are seen as a legalistic-conservative elite that has traditionally protected the status quo and has reproduced the role of the judge as the mouthpiece of the law (Couso, 2010; Hilbink, 2007). Likewise, the judiciary is recognized as one of the most bureaucratic and hierarchical institutions within Latin American political systems (Pásara, 2010). The reproduction of this legalistic behavior is characterized by judges who follow the principle of legality and restrict their jurisdictional activity to what is written in the law (González-Ocantos, 2016).

With this image in mind, can we anticipate judges harnessing their authority to propel social and political-democratic progress? Do they behave like policy makers? Over the past few decades, research in the field of judicial politics has revealed that courts have increased their involvement in resolving significant political and social issues. Consequently, the concepts of judicial activism and the judicialization of politics have gained prominence in discussions (Sieder et al., 2005; Stone 2000; Guarnieri & Pederzoli, 2002). Many of the works that have been written provide different explanations to judicial bahavior. Strategic explanation of judicial behavior indicate that judicial decision making is largely driven by rational calculations, preferences, the strategic interests of judges in response to the institutional context in which they are inserted, as well as the expected choices that other relevant actors (legislators or judges) would make (Epstein & Knight, 1998; Helmke, 2004). In fact, Epstein and Knight called the emergence of this approach the "strategic revolution" in judicial politics (2000). Another approach to explaining judicial behavior, which has dominated the study of courts in the United States is the attitudinal model. This approach indicates that judges decide cases on a liberal-conservative continuum following their sincere ideological stances and the dynamics of the case (Segal & Spaeth, 1993). In these approaches, the role of cultural and ideational factors in judges' decision making is minimized. In fact, few studies in judicial politics have considered that these factors play an important role in the behavior of judges. Scholars following this approach pay a lot of attention to endogenous factors, such as ideas, values, attitudes, beliefs, practices, or the professional socialization of judges (Hilbink, 2007; Couso, 2010; Couso & Hilbink, 2011; Nunes, 2010; Ingram, 2016b; González-Ocantos, 2016; Robinson & Swedlow, 2018; Ansolabehere et al., 2023). In general, these studies affirm that judicial behavior can also be shaped by the legal culture of judges and the legal preferences or understanding that judges have of the law—that is, the judges' views on the sources of law and how it should be applied, interpreted, reasoned, and justified (González-Ocantos, 2016), as well as their ideas about the relationship between law and morality or law and politics.

The legal culture of judges then seems to be a relevant factor for judicial decision making. Judges are a disciplined elite formed in different legal-philosophical traditions (see Chapter 2) that nourish their ideas, values, attitudes, and beliefs at different times and in different institutional environments during their professional career. For example, candidates to the bench shape their legal culture in law school through the subjects they learn—and the way they learn them—(Aguiar-Aguilar & Torres, 2022; Lista & Brigido, 2002), and in daily interaction with their professors (many of them judges), when they start working for other judges in the court and are immersed in the rituals and procedures imposed by the institution (Bárcena, 2018), when they re-engage with the academic legal community by attending seminars or studing for a master's or a doctorate, or when they get involved in judicial associations or work closely with sociolegal networks (González-Ocantos, 2016). Within these institutions and actors in the judicial realm, judges are socialized with understandings about specific ideas on how the law should be applied, the values that are appropriate within the judicial community, the attitudes that are rewarded within the judiciary, or the beliefs about the role that judges are expected to play during their careers. These ideas, values, attitudes, and beliefs of what it is to be a judge do not disappear once they sit on their court, but they develop, reproduce, reinforce, and remain an important asset for deciding cases. Therefore, the concept of legal culture contributes to understanding the shared interpretations of judges about the law and their role in politics and society, which in turn makes it possible to capture relevant attributes of judicial behavior that strategic theories do not capture when they focus only on the rational calculations of judges.

In this sense, we could expect to see different types of rulings depending on the types of legal culture that judges have. On the one hand, judges may have positivist ideas, values, attitudes, and beliefs. In this case, we can expect to find a judge who helps to preserve the status quo and whose sentences hinder the expansion of rights that are not positivized, that is, enshrined in the constitution of legal norms. This type of judge is characterized by mechanically applying what is written in the constitution, avoiding any moral interpretation in their reasoning that could change the meaning of the law enacted by the legislator. In summary, judges close to the positivist tradition believe that they cannot change the law because they are not political actors, but an apolitical elite. On the other hand, the ideas, values, attitudes, and beliefs of judges can be of an argumentative constitutionalist type, contributing to building cases that change the status quo. Here we can expect to find judges who interpret the law using their ideas, values, and beliefs in decision making, weighing up the rights that are in conflict with the current legislation. Judges with an argumentative constitutionalist legal culture recognize and make use of their legislative and political role to shape the law and change the status quo when facing difficult cases; they are defenders of judicial activism. It is important to note that these are two ideal types of legal culture and, in practice, judges may shift between these positions as circumstances and contexts demand.

This chapter elucidates the prevailing legal culture among Mexican judges: do they consider themselves political actors with a legislative role? Do they consider that judicial decision making can be influenced by social values? These questions are relevant since the legal culture of judges tells us if they will be willing to interpret and reform the law to decide difficult cases in which rights and freedoms are at stake or if they will mechanically apply the current legislation and, in this way, protect the enacted law and the status quo. In addition, by answering these questions, one of the least-studied aspects in the literature of judicial politics is addressed: the legal culture of judicial elites. In the following section, the evidence collected in the survey with judges of the federal judiciary is presented, particularly the part related to their perspectives and positions on the premises developed by positivism and argumentative constitutionalism. Also, to evaluate the type of legal culture that judges have, their opinions on controversial issues such as abortion or the decriminalization of drugs are discussed. In some of these topics, the Supreme Court has delivered significant judgments, while in others, it has not, providing an opportunity to discern whether the judges' inclinations lean more toward aligning with matters already settled by the Supreme Court (positivists) or toward crafting interpretations (argumentative constitutionalists) grounded in their genuine ideas or beliefs on the matter. The third section presents two descriptive statistical analyses to corroborate the types of legal culture we found among the judges. The last section presents some tentative conclusions.

The Political Role of Judges: Between Legalism and Argumentative Constitutionalism

The idea that judges are political actors is well known in the literature on judicial politics, at least since 1963, when Martin Shapiro urged the political and legal communities to recognize this fact in his seminal article "Political jurisprudence." Judges, but also lawyers and legal scholars, in Latin American countries may think that this idea is controversial, as it is widely believed that judges should be isolated from politics to deliver impartial, independent, and objective rulings (Pásara, 2010), but also to avoid violating the majority principle of democracy (Waldron, 2018). One significant implication of judges perceiving themselves as political actors is the significance they attribute to their rulings in terms of controlling or constraining government actions, shaping citizens' rights, reshaping public policies, and guiding societal transformations. It is crucial to acknowledge the potential impact that judges can wield within the political system since they actively partake in this process (Shapiro, 1964: 296–297; Guarnieri 2003). Thus, we can expect that judges who believe they have a legislative role or who are relevant actors in the political arena will push their ideas and values through their rulings.

Throughout their legal education in Mexico, judges have primarily been immersed in positivist theories. In law schools, judges have been taught and socialized to the idea that the legitimate source of law is the legislative authority, emphasizing the separation of law and morality. Accordingly, they have been instructed to apply the law rather than engage in the evaluation of various principles when rendering judgments. These ideas are reinforced during their professional careers in the courts, where the judicial career is partially guaranteed if the style and criteria of superior judges are reproduced (Bárcena, 2018). As in other countries (particularly in Latin America and Southern Europe), this began to change in recent decades due to the diffusion and internalization of international human rights law and the introduction of argumentative constitutionalist theories (Couso, 2010: 148–149; Guarnieri, 2003: 156–157; Ansolabehere et al., 2023), but also with the aim of complying with the requirement to make legal education less dogmatic and more practical (Brígido & Lista, 2009: 327). In light of this context, the judicial elites in Mexico have traditionally been categorized as positivists. Consequently, one would anticipate encountering a majority of judges who disavow any active political role, exhibit deference to the legislature, and assert a distinct separation between law and morality. It is conceivable that only a minority of judges, often the younger ones, may embrace an argumentative constitutionalist legal culture.

The data collected in Mexico reveal a division among judges concerning their perception of their political role. Judges can be categorized into two groups: those who view themselves as political actors and those who hold the belief that judges should maintain an apolitical stance. However, it can be said, that the majority of the sample believes that judges are participants in the political process, meaning that they are willing to be active in policy making. Hence, nearly half of the respondents (43%) strongly agreed with the statement that "Judges are political actors, that is, they are indirectly policy makers" (Graph 6.1). If we also include those who "agree" with this notion, we find that approximately 60% of the sample perceive themselves as "political actors." Only about 25% of judges in Mexico denied the idea of being indirectly policy makers (the categories "strongly disagree" and "disagree"), while around 12% had a neutral position.

When judges were asked to articulate their preference regarding the statement "In current democracies, judges have a legislative role," the inclusion of the term "legislative" appears to have caused a slight reduction in their inclination to select the response "totally agree" (Graph 6.1). Despite this, a significant proportion of judges (60%) in the sample hold beliefs that are closer to an argumentative constitutionalist legal culture and would be willing to be less deferential to representatives and the president, interpreting legislation to promote their ideas when making rulings. Around 40% of the judges in the sample strongly disagreed, disagreed, or held a neutral position regarding the idea that judges have a legislative role—that is, we can observe here the persistence of a legal culture that demands a separation between politics and law, or the ideas or values of judges and the law, as postulated by legal positivism. These findings run contrary to the initially expected outcome, indicating a shift toward an argumentative constitutionalist culture.

Judges in Mexico do not feel comfortable expressing their political ideology. As shown in Graph 6.2, 66% of them prefer to be positioned in the center of the political spectrum, adopt a neutral stance, or do not show political preference between the left and right. This aligns with a positivist legal culture that strives to maintain a clear demarcation between politics and law. Judges do not demonstrate an ideological preference, being consistent with one of the central tenets of positivism,

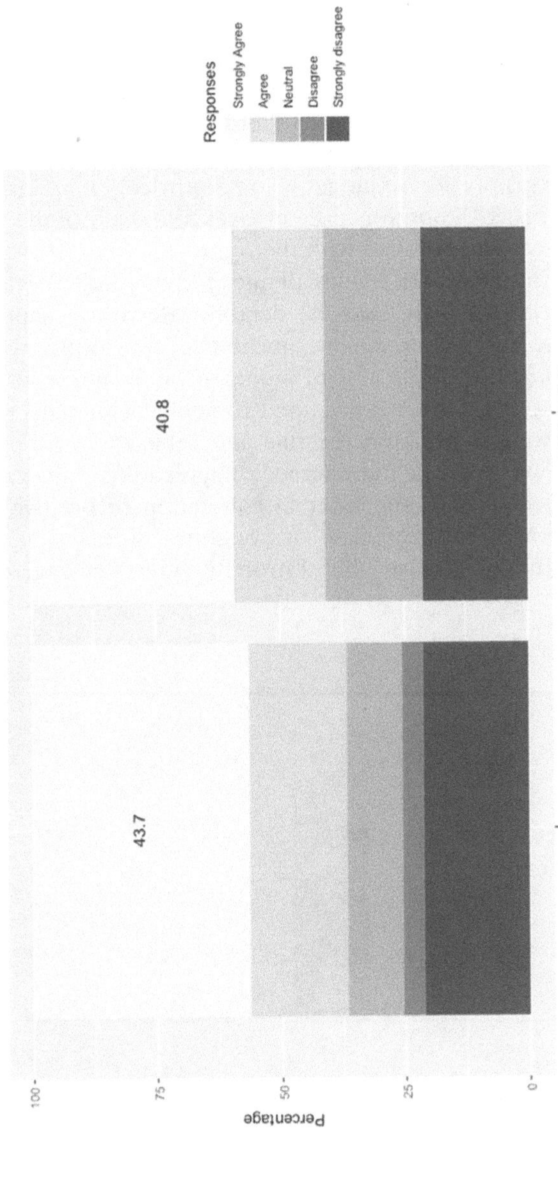

Graph 6.1 Judges as political actors (*Source* Judicial power Database in Mexico, 2019)

which underscores the separation of law from moral, political, or ideological inclinations. The judge is there to make rulings, not to take political stances, several positivists would affirm. In fact, federal judges in Mexico have always shown concern that they might be identified with some party or political position (Ingram, 2019), and publicly deny having ideological preferences. In the Mexican legal tradition, the prevailing notion is that politics should remain separate from judicial activities. This is also confirmed by the proportion of judges who acknowledged having certain political preferences: 18% positioned themselves to the left of the political spectrum, whereas 15% identified with the right.

Referring to the ideas and values of judges regarding the law (see Chapter 2), the judges in the sample demonstrate robust support for concepts that are integral to an argumentative constitutionalist legal culture. Graph 6.3 shows that 85% of judges strongly agreed or agreed with the idea that "judges are not limited to applying the law, they use their creative powers to establish the rule applicable to a case" (JudgesCreativity). Likewise, 90% strongly agreed or agreed that "judges should not limit their decisions to the strict interpretation of positive law, as they have the power to create law by weighing different principles" (LawCreation). Judges also say they "strongly agree" or "agree" with

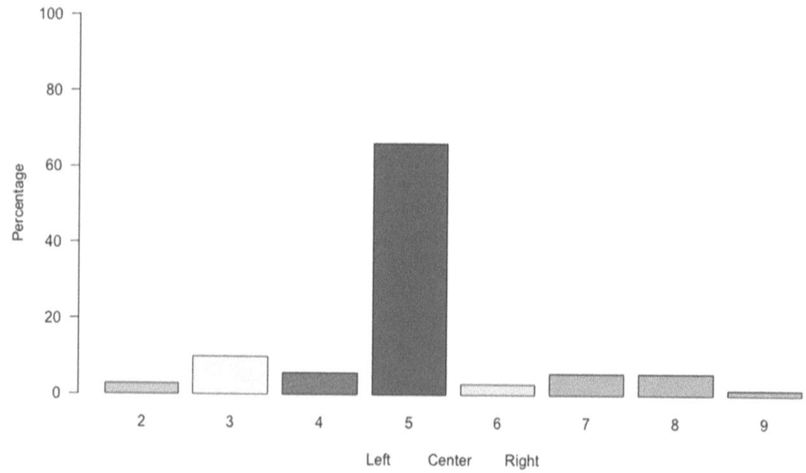

Graph 6.2 Judges' political preferences (*Source* Judicial Power Database in Mexico, 2019)

argumentative constitutionalism ideas such as "Constitutional norms are always subject to weighing and not to direct or automatic application. They can be weighed with principles reasoned by judges when there is a conflict between them" (Weighing) and "The Law has both an authoritative and axiological dimension" (LawAsValue). What this tells us is that the majority of judges would be willing to use their ideas—but also their power—to shape the law when they believe it necessary to do so. Thus, the law is important, but judges are aware and comfortable with the idea that their interpretation can create new rules—in other words, they can legislate from the bench.

However, even if judges are willing to use their ideas and power to shape the law, only 59% of them strongly disagreed or disagreed with the idea that "All constitutional norms are fair" (ConstitutionalNormsAreFair), and 41% strongly agreed or agreed. Thus, an important proportion of judges tended to align here with a positivist legal culture. Judges would have approached an argumentative constitutionalist legal culture if the majority totally disagreed with the idea that "all constitutional norms are fair," since the sole authority of the legislative power is not enough to guarantee that the norms are fair, even in current constitutional democracies. As Gustavo Zagrebelsky has stated, "in the inflated legislative atmosphere of today, there is an abundance of defective, ambiguous, generic, contradictory, irrational and incoherent laws" (2003: 623) that deviate from the idea of justice.

Within an argumentative constitutionalist legal culture, the interpretation and weighing of principles and norms are fundamental elements of the adjudicative process. When judges were questioned about their approach to delivering judgments, approximately 88% of them indicated a preference for "making decisions after weighing the valid constitutional norms and principles in challenging cases" in their capacity as judges rather than "make a decision based on just principles" (7%) or "obey the law and issue a decision based solely on what is written in the constitution" (5%) (see Graph 6.4). During our fieldwork, it became apparent that judges tended to exercise caution when discussing "moral principles" and were reluctant to do so. This behavior contradicts the expectations put forward by constitutional law theories based on principles. When we asked the judges about their perspective on incorporating "moral principles" alongside "principles" in the option of "making a decision after weighing the valid constitutional norms and (moral) principles in difficult cases," several expressed confusion and disagreed with the notion. As

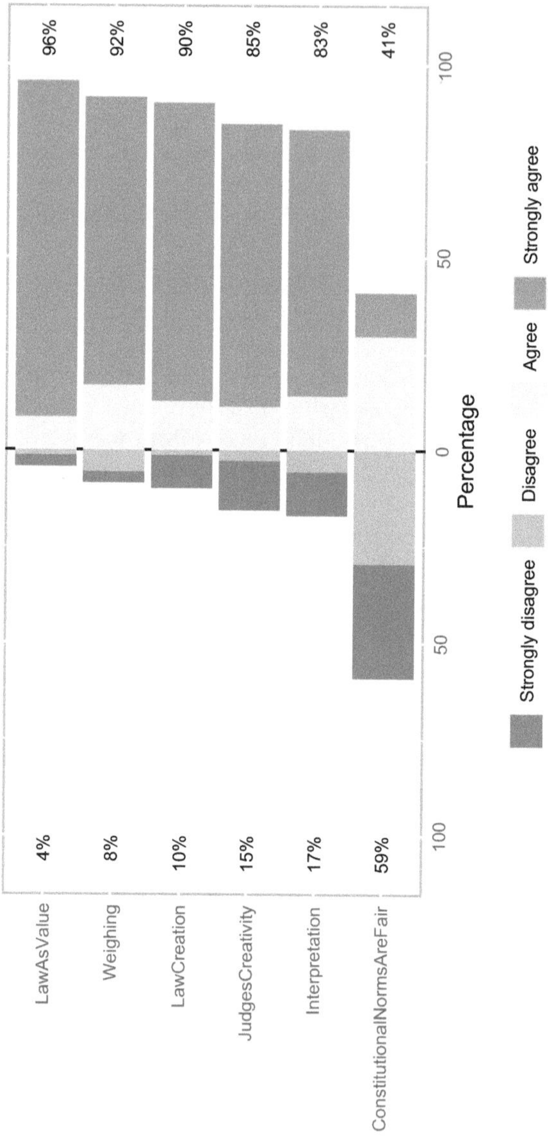

Graph 6.3 Judges' legal ideology (*Source* Judicial Power Database in Mexico, 2019)

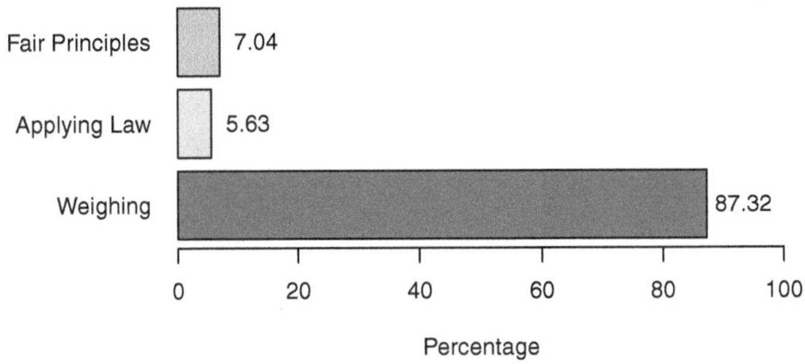

Graph 6.4 Weighing, principles and strict application of the law (*Source* Judicial Power Database in Mexico, 2019)

one judge noted, "a judge's personal morality should not be integrated into a judgment." This illustrates that morality remains a controversial idea associated not with ethics as a universal principle (as proposed by argumentative constitutionalism), but with subjective moral values or opinions.[1]

As discussed in Chapter 2, in a constitutionalist legal culture, judges should consider principles and rules when writing their judgments. Therefore, we can expect judges to weigh up their own ideas about specific principles and those acquired (or shared with) others in their communities when deciding in difficult cases—that is, we can expect them to accept the fact of being influenced by their contexts. We asked judges several questions about various factors that influence judicial decision making, such as national law (NatLaw), national law and value-based criteria (Law&Val), conventional law (ConvLaw), their contact with the parties involved during the judicial process (ConPar), the needs of society (SocNeed), community values (ComVal), and the criteria or thesis of the Supreme Court (SCCriteria). We also inquired about the significance they attributed to subjective factors, such as the viewpoints of esteemed legal professionals (OpJR), the media (OpMe), law makers (OpLeg), the executive (OpEx), and the opinions of society (OpSoc). What Graph 6.5 below shows is that judges have a strong preference (between 60 and 90%) for factors related to what is already legislated or decided by the court: national law, conventional norms, and the criteria of the Supreme Court. It is remarkable that the surveyed judges exhibit a strong consensus on the importance of giving substantial weight to the jurisprudence of the Supreme Court in crafting their judgments. This aligns with the Supreme Court's stance, which has decreed that its jurisprudence is obligatory for lower-level judges (SCJN, 2013), and, as several of them argued during the survey, they can be sanctioned if they do not follow it. Some judges, however, also admitted that they can draft a sentence that justifies well why they are not applying on that occasion a particular Supreme Court criterion with which they do not agree—for example, when the case being decided has relevant differences with the one that formulated the jurisprudence issued by the Supreme Court. However, this idea is supported only by about 10% of the judges included in the sample.

Graph 6.5 also illustrates that judges have less preference (between 0 and 40%) for factors that could be related with the ideas, values, and beliefs that others in their community have about a case that is being decided. Hence, one could contend that when formulating their rulings, judges primarily take into account the law and their individual interpretive framework, but they are less receptive to embracing the viewpoints, values, and perspectives of others within their community, including the parties directly involved in the case under consideration. In Graph 6.5 we can also observe that judges strongly reject the idea of taking into consideration the opinions of the executive (OpEx), the media (OpMed), and law makers (OpLeg) when drafting a sentence.

Many of these ideas, values, and beliefs are consistent with a positivist legal culture, but above all with the particular conception that judges have about judicial independence. In other words, these judges have been educated and trained, and have cultivated their professional experience within a legal community that upholds the belief that judges ought to render decisions regardless of political considerations, societal influences, or external demands. They adhere to the notion that this approach ensures the attainment of impartial, objective, and independent verdicts. Ultimately, this behavior ensures that the principle of legality prevails. Thus, notions of independence and impartiality of judges are equated with apoliticism. In fact, when conducting the surveys, a judge told us that he would not take into account the values or opinions that a particular community has about a case because people have different values, so what could be appropriate for some groups (for example, the adoption of children by LGBTI + couples) might not be for others. Consequently, he

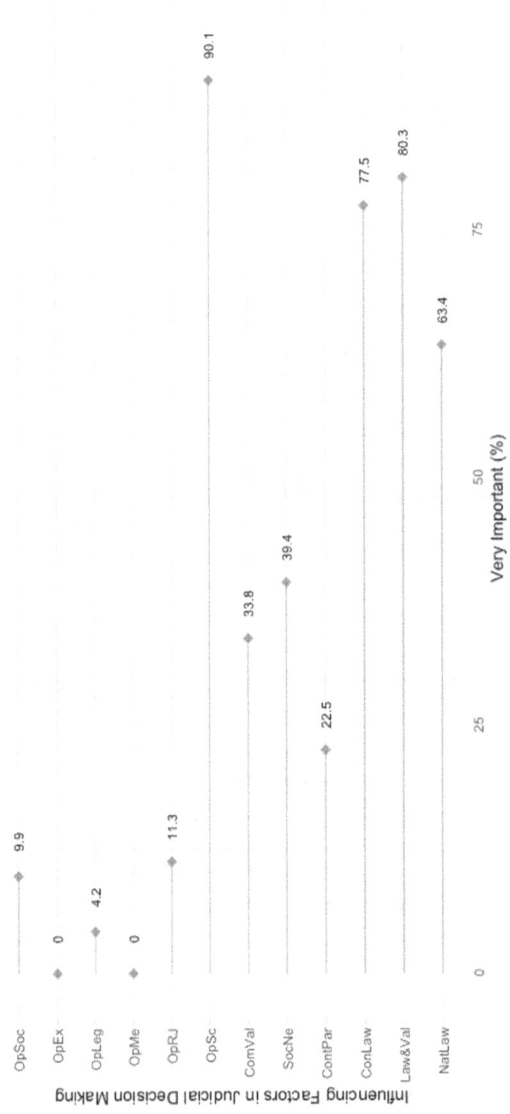

Graph 6.5 When making judgments, how important is it to you…? (*Source* Judicial Power Database in Mexico, 2019)

preferred to leave out of his decisions the values, ideas, and opinions of others, including affected groups or individuals.

Another way for gauging whether judges are willing to utilize their authority to transform the status quo involves assessing their stances on contentious topics within the public agenda, including issues such as same-sex marriage, abortion, the legalization of marijuana, or the decriminalization of drugs. In this context, Mexican judges exhibit diverse preferences, although, as a general trend, they tend to align with the progressive end of the political and rights spectrum, but also to a positivist legal culture. Graph 6.6 below shows that around 90% of the judges in the sample strongly agreed with the idea of LGBTI+ individuals having the right to marry, 53% strongly agreed with a woman's right to legally terminate her pregnancy, while 45% strongly agreed with the legalization of marijuana. The respondents, however, strongly disagreed (25%), disagreed (43%) or have a neutral position (around 30%) regarding the "decriminalization of drug use in general," that is, abolishing penalties for drug use. When we consider the first three statements, it is plausible to argue that judges generally exhibit progressive ideas and values, which could serve as a foundation for decisions that safeguard minority rights. Nonetheless, it is important to note that in recent years, the Supreme Court has issued significant decisions related to same-sex marriage, abortion, and the legalization of marijuana. However, there are no legislative or judicial precedents regarding the decriminalization of drugs. This implies that judges tend to behave more like law enforcers rather than policy makers. They are inclined to align with rights and freedoms that have already been established by the legislature or the Supreme Court, in contrast to issues lacking precedent from a higher authority, which is characteristic of a positivist legal culture.

As can be seen, Mexican judges exhibit various forms of legal culture, reflecting a diverse range of perspectives, values, and attitudes within the judiciary, in some cases they align more with an argumentative constitutionalist legal culture, but in others, positivist positions still persist. To validate and reinforce these findings, the next section conducts both a factor analysis and a hierarchical cluster analysis using the legal culture variables in the Judicial Power in Mexico database.

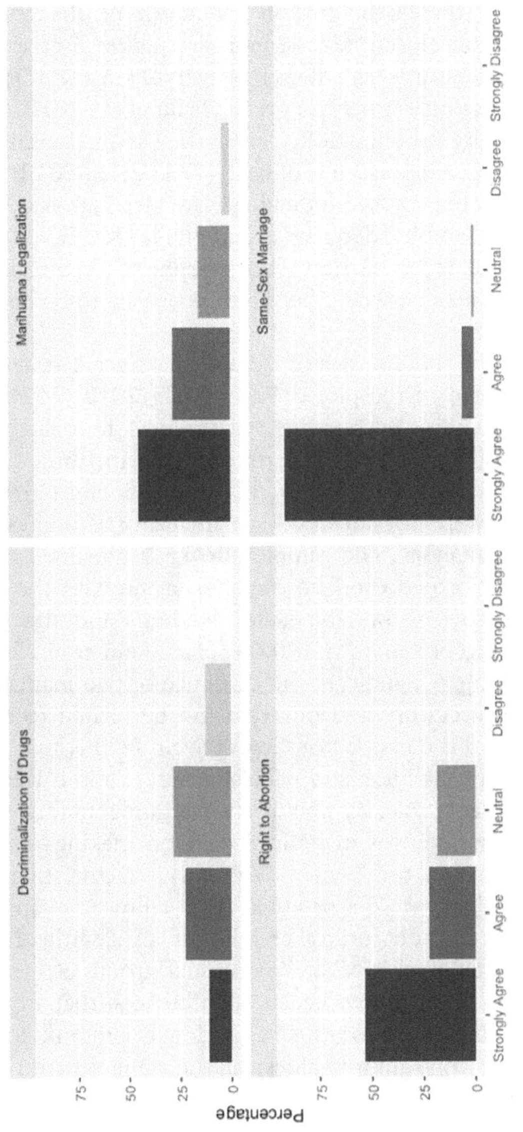

Graph 6.6 Ideas about rights and freedoms (*Source* Judicial Power Database in Mexico, 2019)

Types of Legal Culture in the Federal Judiciary

Prior to conducting the factor analysis to determine the quantity and nature of legal cultures among federal judiciary judges, I carried out—as suggested by the literature—the Kaiser–Meyer–Olkin (KMO) measurement to verify if the sample was appropriate (Field et al., 2012: 769–770). Of the 25 legal culture variables collected in the survey, I excluded seven that were below the acceptable limit of 0.50 (Field et al., 2012: 795). The KMO measures selected for the individual variables had values between 0.52 and 0.78. The sample adequacy is acceptable: KMO = 0.7. Subsequently, I also conducted a Bartlett's test of sphericity (Murphy, 2021), in which the correlations between the variables proved to be high enough for factor analysis.

Later, to determine the number of factors to extract, I tested different techniques such as the "scree plot" (Field et al., 2012: 762) and principal component analysis. Both suggested three to four factors for the analysis. An initial factor analysis was performed with three factors and oblique rotation ("oblimin").[2] From this result, I omitted four additional variables that were not above 0.4 on any factor as suggested by the literature in factor analysis. The sample adequacy remained acceptable: KMO = 0.73. I performed the factor analysis again with the remaining 14 variables. Table 6.1 shows the factor loadings and the p-value of 0.144—above the acceptable limit of 0.05 (Hartmann et al., 2018).

The results in Table 6.1 indicate the existence of two main features of constitutionalist legal culture and one that can be related to a positivist legal culture. I named the first factor "legislative role" because it includes variables that evaluate the ideas and beliefs of judges about their political and legislative (indirect) role, as well as their argumentation, weighting, and interpretation preferences in judicial decision making—in short, to potentially legislate from the bench. Within this factor, there are two negative loads, which measure a positivist legal culture, meaning a position in which judges consider judicial creation of law illegitimate. I named the second factor "post-positivist role" because it groups elements related to considerations beyond the law (i.e. social influences) that are important to judges when making a decision, such as society's opinions, contact with the parties involved, community values, or the opinions of a renowned jurist. As discussed in the second section, this is closer to a constitutionalist legal culture. The third factor, "legalistic role," reveals a positivist position. The loads above 0.4 are variables that reflect to what extent

Table 6.1 Factor Analysis: variables of legal culture

Rotated factor loads of Oblimin

	Legislative role	*Post-positivist role*	*Legalist role*
Judges have a legislative role	0.460	0.184	−0.230
Judges create and develop norms	0.58		−0.206
Judges do not limit themselves to applying the law; they use their creative powers to establish the applicable standard	0.861		
Judges should not create rules, only apply the existing law	−0.578	0.174	0.147
Judges act illegitimately when they interpret and introduce a new law	−0.679		−0.18
Judges are not limited to interpreting the rules of positive law, but are also empowered to create rules themselves	0.739		0.107
When writing a decision, how important is it to you: conventional standards			0.690
When writing a decision, how important is it to you: contact with the involved parties		0.696	−0.149
When writing a decision, how important is it to you: the needs of society		0.664	
When writing a decision, how important is it to you: community values regarding the case		0.734	
When writing a decision, how important is it to you: the criteria of the Supreme Court		−0.105	0.496
When drafting a decision, how important is it to you: the criteria of International Courts			0.669
When writing a decision, how important is it to you: the opinion of a renowned jurist		0.549	0.256
When writing a decision, how important is it to you: the opinions of society		0.659	
	Legislative Role	Post-positivist Role	Legalistic Role
SS Loadings	2.661	2.285	1.421
Proportion of Variance	0.19	0.163	0.102
Accumulated Variance	0.19	0.353	0.455
Test of the hypothesis that 3 factors are sufficient			
The chi-square statistic is 62.83 with 52 degrees of freedom			
The p-value is 0.144			

Source Judicial Power Database in Mexico, 2019

judges are supporters of following the rules, showing high consideration for the legal criteria established by the Supreme Court, international courts, and international treaties—that is, for what is already ruled by courts or legislated by state representatives.[3] Likewise, we can see some negative signs in the variables that measure the positions of a constitutionalist legal culture. The *SS Loadings* are above the acceptable limit of 1 (Hartmann et al., 2018), so I use the three factors for the subsequent analysis. It is worth noting that I obtained the factor scores using the "Bartlett" method to construct an index of legal culture variables that could be used to correlate with ideological and demographic variables.

Subsequently, I conducted a Cronbach's reliability test to verify how closely related the elements included in the factor analysis were. The alpha of this test was 0.82, which shows good reliability (above 0.7) among the six variables that make up factor 1 (legislative role); therefore, we can be confident that these variables are consistent. For the five variables with higher loads in factor 2 (post-positivist role) the alpha test was 0.79, which also illustrates the reliability of internal consistency. The alpha test for factor 3 (legalistic role) was 0.65 (a modest level of reliability). Finally, the reliability test for the 14 variables included in the factor analysis had an alpha of 0.78. Therefore, it can be argued that the variables are consistent.

Thus, from the analysis, it can be concluded that the data show that two of the factors group together in what in this work is called argumentative constitutionalist legal culture, while the last factor accounts for the existence of a positivist legal culture, as the descriptive statistics of the previous section also show.

An additional analysis that aids in comprehending and validating the various legal cultures present among federal judges is cluster analysis. I conducted a hierarchical cluster analysis to determine the number of clusters that group distinct types of legal cultures among the judges.

In the analysis, I utilized 12 variables (see below Table 6.2) designed to gauge the attributes and features of legal culture prevalent among judges. To carry out the analysis, missing values were first omitted. Then, dissimilarity values were calculated with Euclidean distance and these values were taken for the analysis. An agglomerative hierarchical cluster was performed and Ward's linkage method was used because it obtains a more balanced grouping structure. Each judge (x-axis) was grouped into a conglomerate based on the response values they provided for each of the 12 variables used for the analysis. We obtained two distinct groups (Fig. 6.1), each with a different number of conglomerates: at a height of

25 (y-axis), the group on the left contains one conglomerate (blue-gray color), while the one on the right contains two groups (turquoise blue and cobalt blue). These three different groups stand out, as each one agglomerates an appropriate size of judges that are useful for conceptual and empirical analysis.

These groups include judges with different types of legal culture. To determine the type of legal culture that judges have in each group, the mean values of each group for the 12 variables included in the cluster analysis were calculated. Judges were identified with a type of positivist-formalist legal culture, others principled-positivist (in the style of Ferrajoli; see Chapter 2), and another more argumentative constitutionalists (see Table 6.2).

The variables were coded on a scale ranging from 1 (totally disagree) to 10 (totally agree). Questions 2, 5, 6, 7, and 10 were positivist-oriented, while the others were argumentative constitutionalist-oriented.

The judges in the formalist-positivist group are those who consider that "all constitutional norms are fair" (7.5) only because they are constitutionalized; they also believe that judicial creation of law is illegitimate (7), since law can only be created by authorized representatives (legislators and the executive). These judges would clearly be classified as legal positivists, but also as false argumentativists. While they deny their role in the judicial creation of the law (4.9) or having a legislative role (3.2), they tend to support the idea of weighing and interpreting the law (8.7), and claim to be surrounded by a network of constitutionalist judges (9.5). In other words, the judges in this category do not want to present themselves as pure formalists, but their ideas do not adequately correspond to an argumentative legal culture.

The judges in the principled-positivist group provided answers that tend to reflect a constitutionalist legal culture, but they were not very convinced of ideas such as that judges are political actors (6.2). They tended to agree more with the idea that judges are apolitical (7) than the formalist-positivists. In addition, the judges in this group tended to be partially deferential to the legislative power, considering that "the norms are fair" given their constitutional rank (5.4). The judges grouped in this category also exhibit some inconsistencies in their responses, although not as pronounced as those among the formalist-positivists. Their stance appears to be more moderate, acknowledging the shortcomings of the classic positivist thesis, but not entirely embracing the role of

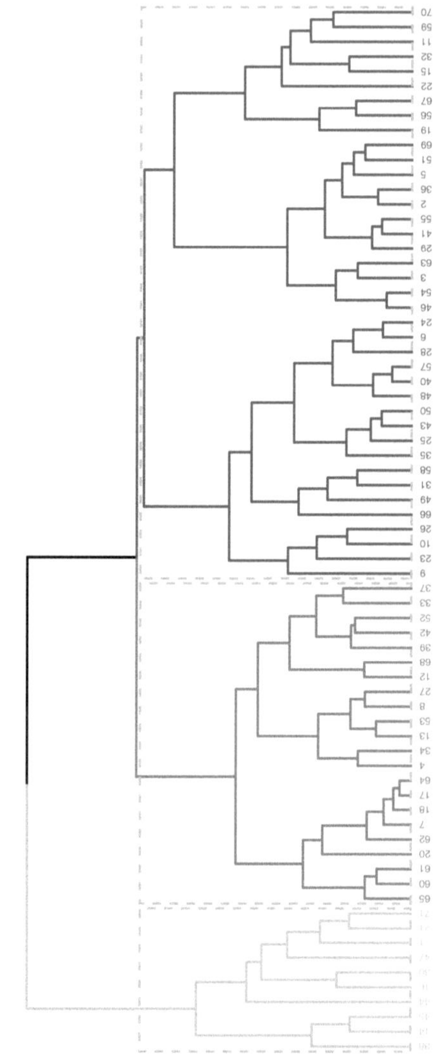

Fig. 6.1 Types of legal culture by judge (*Source* Judicial Power Database in Mexico 2019)

Table 6.2 Configurations of the type of legal culture of the judges (group means)

	Formalist-positivist	*Positivist-constitutionalist*	*Post-positivist*
1. Judges are political actors	5.9	6.6	7.2
2. Judges are apolitical	6.5	7.0	2.1
3. Judges have a legislative function	3.2	7.6	6.3
4. Creativity in the development of judicial norms	2.7	9.1	9.6
5. Strictly apply the law	5.8	1.8	1.7
6. All constitutional norms are fair	7.5	5.4	3.5
7. Positivist judicial network	2.7	4.6	2.0
8. Constitutional judicial network	9.5	7.9	9.6
9. Weighing of the law1	8.7	7.8	8.9
10. Judicial creation of the law is illegitimate	7.0	2.3	1.2
11. Weighing of the law2	8.6	8.8	9.6
12. Creation of judicial law	4.9	9.4	9.3

Source Judicial Power Database in Mexico (2019)

the argumentative constitutionalist judge who carefully considers principles, provides legal reasoning that can shape law, and actively participates in the realm of rights-based politics.

The judges in the argumentative constitutionalist group tend to define themselves as political actors (7.2) with the power to create law (9.3) and weigh up different principles (9.6). They also categorically reject the idea that judges should mechanically apply the law (1.7), or that the judicial creation of law is illegitimate (1.2), as well as that all constitutional norms are fair (3.5). This category of judges is the furthest from the classical thesis of legal positivism and most accurately represent the thesis of argumentative constitutionalism, favoring the activism of judges in the judicial creation of norms (9.6).

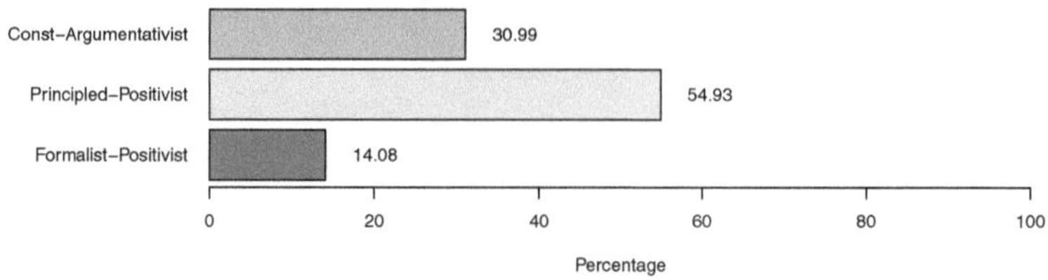

Graph 6.7 Types of culture in the Federal Judicial Power of Mexico (*Source* Judicial Power Database in Mexico [2019])

Surprisingly, it was discovered that the largest proportion of judges (55%) fell into the principled-positivist category. In contrast to initial expectations, the second most substantial group comprised judges with a constitutionalist-argumentative legal culture (31%) (as depicted in Graph 6.7). Finally, slightly over an eighth of our sample (14%) was clustered into the formalist-positivist category, which aligns more closely with a conventional positivist legal perspective.

Based on these data, we could say that almost 70% (principled-positivist and formalist-positivist) of federal judges in Mexico retain key aspects of legal positivism, like denying the active role that judges play in the political arena, but they have also acquired several characteristics of argumentative constitutionalism such as weighing norms and principles when deciding complex cases.

Thus, the legal culture of judges in Mexico reveals that despite the notion that argumentative ideas could be gaining ground, the positivist type legal culture remains robust and alive among judges. Recently, this finding has also been confirmed by another study (Ansolabehere et al., 2023). We encounter judges who, at times, opt to restrict their decisions to what is explicitly stated in the law, whereas in other instances, they are willing to engage in judicial law making (shaping the law through interpretation). There are judges who accept that they are political actors, but deny having a political preference. What is even more significant is that specific judges exhibit progressive inclinations and opinions concerning rights and freedoms. This can potentially engender heightened societal expectations regarding the safeguarding of rights and the imposition of well-defined constraints by the judiciary on the "tyranny of the majority." However, their legal culture follows the positivist tradition showing deference toward the Supreme Court and toward legislation, in addition to many of them considering the social influences in judicial decision making to be controversial. In this context, it is conceivable to encounter cases that, albeit infrequently, protect and champion rights, yet also numerous ones that, as seen in preceding decades, uphold the existing state of affairs, particularly in complex cases. Future research that takes as a basis the rulings issued by judges on issues that claim rights for disadvantaged groups such as women, migrants, rural workers, indigenous peoples, or the LGBTI + community would help to better inform this hypothesis.

Conclusions

The aim of this chapter was to better understand the type of legal culture that prevails among the judicial elite in Mexico. From the data we learned that the judges of the federal judiciary in Mexico show that, despite the fact that argumentative constitutionalism is gaining ground, legal positivism still guides the ideas, values, attitudes, and beliefs of judges. The judges do not widely (or publicly) assume their political role or their power to shape the law, so we cannot expect to see an activist judiciary whose judges frequently alter the paths of the political and social arena. Attitudes are still dominated by a hierarchy in which we find certain institutions perceived as the most legitimate sources of judicial decision making: legislation or the jurisprudence of the Supreme Court are considered extremely important in determining the fairness of a norm, but also the preferences for freedoms and social rights that judges are eager to promote. Over 20 years since the introduction of constitutionalist legal theories into legal education and the legal profession, a noteworthy proportion of judges still adhere to the principle of judicial restraint and perceive their role primarily as the "mouthpiece" of the law, rejecting the notion that they act as policy makers through the judiciary. The key implication of these findings is that we can anticipate a continuation of judges who lean toward a mechanical application of the law in their judgments.

In conclusion, the empirical findings presented in this chapter resonate not only within the context of Mexico but also with judiciaries in other nations, particularly in the Ibero-American region, where positivism and, more recently, argumentative constitutionalism have served as the foundations, to differing extents, for legal education and practice. Understanding the scope and predominance of these legal paradigms will allow us to better understand the legal culture of judges in terms of how much they consider themselves political actors or an apolitical elite.

This contributes to clarifying the key internal factors underlying judicial activism or restraint and advancing the debate seeking to explain judicial behavior.

Notes

1. I thank Ilsse Torres Ortega for pointing out this point.
2. Oblique rotation is recommended when theory suggests that the factors in the analysis could be correlated (Field et al., 2012: 789–791). In this case, the factors could be correlated because they are grouping questions into two dimensions: (a) the legal ideas of the judges; and (b) the beliefs of the judges when drafting judicial decisions.
3. The use of conventional norms (treaties signed by the state) and the criteria of international courts when drafting judicial sentences can also be considered a constitutionalist feature because the judges go beyond positive national law. Therefore, this factor could group together contradictory variables.

Bibliography

Aguiar-Aguilar, A., & Torres, I. (2022). Explaining the Sources of Judges' Legal Conceptions in the Mexican Judiciary. *Latin American Law Review, 9*, 117–137.

Ansolabehere, K., Botero S., & González-Ocantos E. (2023). Conceptualizing and Measuring Legal Culture. Evidence from a Survey of Mexican Federal Judges. *Politics and Government*. CIDE.

Bárcena, E. (2018). Judicial Reproduction and Legal Culture. The System of Appointment of Personnel in the Mexican Supreme Court. *Oñati Socio-legal Series*, *8*(5), 739–759.

Couso, J. (2010). The Transformation of Constitutional Discourse and the Judicialization of Politics in Latin America. In J. Couso, A. Huneeus, & R. Sieder (Eds.), *Cultures of Legality: Judicialization and Political Activism in Latin America* (pp. 141–160). Cambridge University Press.

Couso, J., & Hilbink, L. (2011). From Quietism to Incipient Activism. In G. Helmke & J. Rios-Figueroa (Eds.), *Courts in Latin America* (pp. 99–127). Cambridge University Press.

Epstein, L., & Knight, J. (1998). *The Choices Justices Make*. Congressional Quarterly Press.

Epstein, L., & Knight, J. (2000). Toward a Strategic Revolution in Judicial Politics: A Look Back. *Political Research Quarterly, 53*(3), 625–661.

Field, A., Miles, J., & Field, Z. (2012). *Discovering Statistics Using R*. Sage Publications Ltd.

González-Ocantos, E. (2016). *Shifting Legal Visions: Judicial Change and Human Rights Trials in Latin America*. Cambridge University Press.

Guarnieri, C. (2003). Giustizia e politica. I nodi della Seconda Repubblica. Roma: Il Mulino.

Guarnieri, C., & Pederzoli, P. (2002). *The Judiciary in Contemporary Democracies*. Editori Laterza.

Hartmann, K., Krois, J., & Waske, B. (2018). *E-Learning Project SOGA: Statistics and Geospatial Data Analysis*. Freie Universitaet Berlin.

Helmke, G. (2004). *Courts Under Constraints: Judges, Generals, and Presidents in Argentina*. Cambridge University Press.

Hilbink, L. (2007). *Judges Beyond Politics in Democracy and Dictatorship: Lessons from Chile*. Cambridge University Press.

Ingram, M. (2016b). Networked Justice: Judges, the Diffusion of Ideas, and Legal Reform Movements in Mexico. *Journal of Latin American Studies, 48*(4), 739–768.

Ingram, M. (2019). Interviews. Judicial Politics in the Voice of the Experts. In A. Aguiar-Aguilar (Ed.), *Government and Judicial Politics in Mexico* (pp. 172–193). Fontamara, IIJ-UNAM, TEPJF.

Lista, C., & Brigido, A. (2002). *The Teaching of Law and the Formation of Legal Consciousness*. Sima Publisher.

Judicial Power Database in Mexico, (2019). Available under request at https://aguiarazul.wordpress.com/contact

Murphy, Phil. (2021). "Exploratory Factor Analysis". Available at: https://rstudio-pubs-static.s3.amazonaws.com/758265_6365231ce6684382a66302e34fe0aeb3.html.

Nunes, R. (2010). Ideational Origins of Progressive Judicial Activism: The Colombian Constitutional Court and the Right to Health. *Latin American Politics and Society, 52*(3), 67–97.

Pásara, L. (2010). *Three Keys to Justice in Peru*. Fondo Editorial de la PUCP.

Robinson, R., & Swedlow, B. (2018). Beyond Liberal and Conservative: Advancing the Study of Judicial Behavior with a Cultural Theory of Political Values. *Journal of Law and Courts, 6*(2), 263–302.

SCJN. (2013). "Contradiction of Thesis 299/2013". *Weekly Judicial of the Federation*. https://sjf.scjn.gob.mx/sjfsist/paginas/DetalleGeneralV2.aspx?id=25944&Clase=DetalleTesisEjecutorias.

Sieder, Rachel, Line Schjolden and Alan Angell. (2005). The judicialization of politics in Latin America. New York: Palgrave Macmillan

Segal, J., & Spaeth, H. (1993). *The Supreme Court and the Attitudinal Model*. Cambridge University Press.

Shapiro, M. (1964). *Law and Politics in the Supreme Court*. The Free Press of Glencoe.

Sweet, S. A. (2000). *Governing with Judges: Constitutional Politics in Europe*. Oxford University Press.

Waldron, J. (2018). *Against the Government of the Judges. Advantages and Disadvantages of Making Decisions by Majority in Congress and in the Courts*. Siglo XXI Editores.

Zagrebelsky, G. (2003). Ronald Dworkin's Principle Based Constitutionalism. *International Journal of Constitutional Law, 1*(4), 621–650.

CHAPTER 7

Concluding Remarks: The Judiciary—A Privileged, Nepotistic, and Formalistic Institution?

Abstract This book has been dedicated to scrutinizing the judiciary from an internal perspective and illuminating whether judges constitute a traditionalist and formalistic elite, or whether they are equipped to safeguard rights and restrain the tyranny of the majority. The judiciary in Mexico have the institutional conditions to do so and this book examines whether judges have or do not have the profiles, ideas, beliefs, and values to advance rights or limit the government. This is of utmost importance, particularly in contexts where attacks on court decisions and their independence have begun to spread. The primary contribution of this work lies in its provision of original data on aspects that include judges' social backgrounds, professional paths, careers, judicial governance, and, notably, their legal culture.

Keywords Legal culture · Judicial career · Professional career · Judges · Social backgrounds

In recent years, we have witnessed judges within the federal judiciary issuing decisions that have altered the political landscape and impacted rights. We have also observed them defending their rulings, career, and independence when faced with criticisms or attacks from the executive

A. A. Aguiar Aguilar, *Legal Culture, Sociopolitical Origins and Professional Careers of Judges in Mexico*,
https://doi.org/10.1007/978-3-031-52909-2_7

branch or the public. They have been branded as a corrupt elite, accused of enabling the release of criminals, and, and in certain instances, we have also witnessed public effigies of judges being burned in protest. Many individuals perceive the judiciary as comprising judges who do not advocate for citizens' interests, receive substantial incomes, and issue judgments that appear to favor the existing order rather than the rights sought in the courtroom.

Amid these events and perceptions, the federal judiciary in Mexico has evolved into a pivotal institution in the legal system and the political regime. It serves as an arena for resolving conflicts between political authorities, with federal judges wielding the authority to refrain from enforcing legislation that runs counter to the Constitution. Non-elected individuals, who attain their positions without universal direct suffrage, can make decisions with substantial political, economic, and social implications for democratic governance and people's lives. Consequently, this book has been dedicated to scrutinizing the judiciary from an internal perspective and illuminating whether judges constitute a traditionalist, and formalistic elite, or whether they are equipped to safeguard rights and restrain the dominance of the majority. The federal judiciary in Mexico has the institutional conditions to balance political power and protect rights and this book accounts for whether judges have or do not have the profiles, ideas, beliefs, and values to do so. This is of utmost importance, particularly in contexts where attacks on court decisions and their independence have begun to spread both in consolidated democracies (like the United States) and in countries with defective democracies (like Mexico and El Salvador).

The research outlined in this book enables us to gain a deeper understanding of one of the least-explored elites of the political system: district and circuit judges in the federal judiciary. The primary contribution of this work lies in its provision of original data on aspects that have received limited attention in the existing literature on judicial politics or legal sociology. These aspects include the judges' social backgrounds, professional paths, careers, judicial governance, and, notably, the prevailing legal culture among the judicial elite responsible for adjudicating rights within the district and circuit courts.

A central aim of this volume was to empirically measure a concept that has been relegated in judicial politics for being "cloudy," "amorphous," and difficult to operationalize: the legal culture of judges (see Chapter 2). Following the introduction of the evolution of studies in judicial politics in Mexico, this book has outlined the theories of judicial behavior that have been employed in these research endeavors: strategic, neoinstitutionalist, attitudinal, and ideational. To construct the concept of legal culture and to contribute to strengthening ideational theories, it was necessary to interweave the proposals of three areas of knowledge: judicial politics, legal sociology, and the philosophy of law. The ideas put forward by the latter were particularly illuminating in terms of capturing the different legal conceptions that nourish the various types of legal culture, as well as determining the indicators contained in the concept and that allow for the observation and empirical measurement of the legal culture of judges. Thus, one of the most important contributions of this book has been to bring together disciplines that sat at separate tables, to paraphrase Almond (1988), and offer a more appropriate understanding and measurement of the concept of legal culture.

Nevertheless, the most significant challenge in pursuing the aforementioned goal was gathering data from a population renowned for being "difficult to survey." The judicial elite is isolated from society and is wary of contact with the public, as judges believe this could cast doubt on their independence or, alternatively, they are conveniently skeptical of the idea that the judiciary should also be accountable and transparent, like any other institution that is financed by public resources. The data that were collected contribute to broadening the study of the judiciary and the legal culture of judges from a different methodological perspective: the survey. Thus, it complements studies that have been developed on these topics using ethnography and qualitative methods (see Chapter 3). Despite the difficulties, one of the important and novel contributions of this research is that it managed to survey face-to-face district judges and electoral magistrates with experience in different circuits, subjects, and of different ages, genders, and careers within the judiciary. The result was a database from which descriptive statistical analyses were derived, enhancing our comprehension of the individuals who make up the judiciary.

The chapters presented in this volume have explored the internal dynamics of the judiciary from various perspectives and have offered additional insights that help us determine whether judges are up to the task of addressing the expectations of a diverse and pluralistic society striving to enhance its rights within a democratic framework.

Thus, we know that the judicial elite in Mexico holds significant influence and substantial wealth, but this assertion requires certain nuances. Judges belong to one of the best-compensated elites; nevertheless, this reflects the outcome of a judicial reform process geared toward constructing a robust institution capable of counterbalancing the other two branches of government and furthering the rights of the citizenry. Contrary to what is commonly thought of judges—for example, that they come from families with illustrious surnames and a longstanding tradition within the judiciary—their social origins primarily trace back to lower-middle-class households, where mothers typically assumed the role of homemakers, while fathers provided for the family. Fathers' occupations spanned two sectors: skilled trades (including carpenters, military personnel, and mechanics) and professions (such as teachers, engineers, and legal practitioners). Consequently, it can be asserted that judges have successfully achieved upward social mobility and do not predominantly come from families with extensive judicial backgrounds. Nevertheless, as demonstrated by other studies (Borrego, 2017; Ríos-Figueroa, 2018), they have managed to establish such familial lineage. This has arisen from the judicial career system that required competitive examinations only for positions as judges and magistrates, but not for the broader category of officials working within the judiciary.

Now, despite having social origins in which they could know and experience levels of inequality and social injustices (see Chapter 4), their training, professional trajectory, and the judicial career they have followed have put them in an isolated and distant position from these problems, and a significant proportion of female and male judges still believe that their decisions should be made without considering other (substantive) aspects beyond what the law stipulates. The implication of this is disheartening, as we could observe how one of the powers authorized to protect and expand the rights of the citizenship and limit the tyranny of the majority abdicates its ability to do so.

Additionally, the data collected for this book reveal the existence of judges who can be referred to as "professionals" by virtue of their career trajectory in the judiciary. Unlike other public sector officials in Mexico, such as state court judges or the type of judges who populated the judiciary prior to the 1994 reform, present-day judges have had to undergo competitive examinations to attain the top two positions within the judicial career: circuit judge and district judge. Judges have undergone a process of professionalization; they have been educated, assessed, and promoted by a judicial governance body that operates independently and holds them accountable (see Chapter 5). Despite this, the data also reveal that the Achilles' heel of the judicial career lies in the way in which access to the lowest ranks is granted. Without having to go through competitive and rigorous contests, but only through the discretionary filter of the head of the court, entry into the judiciary gave rise to a nepotistic and clientelistic network that—combined with the design of the contests for the highest positions—effectively closed the doors of the judiciary to candidates who did not have family or friendship ties with the inhabitants of the judiciary. This should begin to change following a judicial reform approved in 2021.

Contrary to expectations, which presumed that the overwhelming majority of judges in Mexico adhere to a positivist legal culture, the data also indicate a growing influence of an argumentative constitutionalist legal culture. This trend is shaping the characteristics of judges and, potentially, the decisions they render (see Chapter 6). A significant proportion of judges are increasingly willing to assume a more active role in policy making and assume that their judicial function has a legislative role. This allows us to affirm that the judiciary is transforming from within, which could have positive implications in terms of having less deferential and more active judges in a political arena where, sometimes, law makers legislate violating the rights of citizens or ignore and despise their demands for better programs and public policies. The data shows that some judges are more willing to "govern" from the bench to avoid the tyranny of the majority in decisions that affect civil rights and political freedoms. However, it is important to note that a noteworthy proportion of judges still adhere to a positivist-formalist legal culture and are averse to the concept of judges being considered political actors who shape the law through their decisions.

One of the key advantages of this book lies in its potential for comparison. The research findings also offer insights into what might occur within the internal dynamics of judiciaries in countries like Mexico, particularly in Latin America. These nations share commonalities, including a civil law legal system, legal education models rooted in the abstract study of laws, judicial and criminal reforms aimed at enhancing the authority and independence of the courts, as well as making rights like due process and the presumption of innocence more robust. Furthermore, they all partake in a process of reshaping legal paradigms with the inclusion of argumentative constitutionalism. Hence, it is feasible to suggest that the circumstances of judges in other countries, such as Argentina, Brazil, and Colombia, exhibit parallel trends to those observed in the study conducted here in terms of the types of legal culture found, sociopolitical origins, social backgrounds, and the transformation and evolution of the model of judicial governance, which still encompasses a variety of practices that can range from a system of recognition, professionalization or discretion for the assignment in some positions.

The research developed in this book lays the groundwork for future lines of research in judicial politics. For instance, it is essential to delve into comparative models examining the shifts within the judiciary based on internal factors like social backgrounds, career paths, legal education, judicial careers, and legal culture. By adopting a comparative approach, researchers can elucidate the intricate interplay between internal factors and judicial behavior within different national contexts. This comparative analysis will facilitate the identification of underlying explanations that shape judicial behavior, thereby enhancing our comprehension of the complexities inherent in the functioning of judiciaries worldwide.

Likewise, it is imperative to examine local judiciaries, about which we currently possess limited or no information, both in Mexico and across Latin America. Studying subnational judiciaries also faces a methodological challenge, particularly in Mexico, as local judicial elites have proven to be less transparent and more hermetic than those at the federal level (Equis Justice, 2021). In the case of Mexico, while accessing information about judiciaries may be challenging, it is evident that aspects such as judicial careers and judicial governance are virtually absent in practice. Instead, clientelistic recruitment systems dominate, undermining the political independence of judges and causing their behavior to mirror the preferences of the local executive in power. The prevalence of clientelistic practices within local judiciaries underscores the urgent need for systematic inquiry and reform efforts aimed at enhancing transparency, accountability, and judicial independence. By shedding light on the inner workings of subnational judiciaries and exposing the underlying mechanisms of influence, scholars and policymakers can work towards fostering a more robust and equitable legal system that upholds the principles of justice and the rule of law.

This work also paves the way for investigating the prevailing legal culture in the rulings rendered by judges. It provides the necessary elements for comparisons, enabling an assessment of whether judges' decisions align with their opinions and self-descriptions in the survey. While in the survey design, attention was given to include various control questions to "unmask a formalist" (to follow Atienza's wording), it should not be dismissed that judges may provide responses that are "socially desirable" or even "politically correct." They may want to depict themselves as argumentative constitutionalists rather than formalist positivists, positioning as judges who promote the rights agenda rather than those who uphold the status quo.

Bibliography

Almond, G. A. (1988). Separate Tables: Schools and Sects in Political Science. *PS: Political Science and Politics, 21* (4), 828–842. https://doi.org/10.2307/420022

Borrego, F. (2017). Study on Family and Client Networks in the Federal Judiciary Council. *Mexican Journal of Justice, 29–30*, 159–191.

Equis Justice. (2021). *Open Justice: From Opacity to Judicial Openness. Ranking of Judicial Transparency in Mexico 2021.* Equis Justice for Women.

Ríos-Figueroa, J. (2018, August 27). The Meritocratic Deficit. Nepotism and Family Networks in the Federal Judicial Power. *Nexos*.

Appendix I

ITESO, Jesuit University of Guadalajara

JUDICIAL POWER AND INDIGENOUS RIGHTS IN MEXICO QUESTIONNAIRE[1]

This questionnaire aims to better understand the judges of the federal judiciary in Mexico: their sociopolitical origins, training, career path and judicial career, and their opinions regarding the role of law in politics and society. This work is part of the Justice Observatory of ITESO, a research project led by professors from the Department of Sociopolitical and Legal Studies (SOJ) of the same institution.

This questionnaire is strictly for academic purposes and guarantees total anonymity of the respondent, so you will not be asked for your name and in the use of the answers no reference will be made to a particular magistrate or judge, but to magistrates and judges. Data will be collected in the states of Nayarit, Jalisco, Puebla, Estado de México, Nuevo León, Ciudad de México, Oaxaca, and Veracruz. The collected data will be used for the publication of academic articles in indexed journals and a book.

A. A. Aguiar Aguilar, *Legal Culture, Sociopolitical Origins and Professional Careers of Judges in Mexico*,
https://doi.org/10.1007/978-3-031-52909-2

Interviewer: Please complete the following information before beginning the survey

Identification data

Collegiate court ____ or District court: _____ No: ____________

Subject matter ____________________ State: ______________________

Circuit: ____

Position of the interviewee: Circuit judge: _____ District judge: ____ Electoral magistrate: ____

Date and time of application: ____________________________

Family and Sociopolitical Origins

FAM1. In which state of the republic were you born?
FAM2. What was your father's main profession?

1. Judge
2. Litigation lawyer
3. Notary
4. Doctor
5. Businessman
6. University professor
7. Engineer
8. Architect
9. Federal government employee
10. State government employee
11. Worker
12. Mechanic
13. Other, which?

FAM3. And your mother's?

1. Judge
2. Lawyer
3. Doctor
4. Notary
5. Businesswoman
6. University professor
7. Engineer
8. Architect
9. Federal government employee

10. State government employee
11. Worker
12. Homemaker
13. Other, which?

FAM4. What is the highest level of education your father completed?

1. Elementary school
2. Middle school
3. High school
4. Bachelor's or professional degree
5. Master's degree
6. PhD

FAM5. What is the highest level of education your mother completed?

1. Elementary school
2. Middle school
3. High school
4. Bachelor's or professional degree
5. Master's degree
6. PhD

FAM6. In which socioeconomic stratum would you classify the household where you grew up?

1. Low stratum
2. Lower middle stratum
3. Middle stratum
4. Upper middle stratum
5. High stratum

FAM7. Have any of your relatives had a career within the judiciary?

1. Yes.
2. No. *If the answer is NO, proceed to question FAM10*

FAM8. Who?

1. Grandfather
2. Grandmother
3. Father
4. Mother

5. Brother or sister
6. Grandfather or grandmother
7. Uncle or aunt
8. Spouse
9. Children
10. Other

FAM9. Have any of your relatives held any elected office?

1. Yes
2. No. *If the answer is NO, proceed to question FAM13*

FAM10. Who?

1. Grandfather
2. Grandmother
3. Father
4. Mother
5. Brother or sister
6. Grandfather or grandmother
7. Uncle or aunt
8. Other

FAM11. What office?

1. Federal deputy
2. Senator
3. Local deputy
4. Municipal president
5. Councilor
6. Governor
7. President of the Republic

FAM12. Do any of your relatives currently hold any elected office?

1. Yes
2. No. *If the answer is NO, proceed to question FAM16*

FAM13. Who?

1. Father
2. Mother
3. Brother or sister
4. Grandfather or grandmother

5. Uncle or aunt
6. Other

FAM14. What office?

1. Federal deputy
2. Senator
3. Local deputy
4. Municipal president
5. Councilor
6. Governor
7. President of the Republic

FAM15. Do any of your relatives belong to a political party?

1. Yes.
2. No. *When the answer is NO, proceed to question FAM18*

FAM16. Who or whom?

1. Father
2. Mother
3. Brother or sister
4. Grandfather or grandmother
5. Uncle or aunt
6. Other

FAM17. Which party?

1. PRI
2. PAN
3. PRD
4. PVEM
5. PT
6. MORENA
7. Citizens' Movement
8. Other, which?

FAM18. Did any of your relatives motivate your decision to pursue a judicial career?

1. Yes
2. No. *When the answer is NO, proceed to question FAM20*

FAM19. Who or whom?

1. Father
2. Mother
3. Brother or sister
4. Grandfather or grandmother
5. Uncle or aunt
6. Other

FAM20. Changing the subject, do you profess any religion?

1. Yes.
2. No. *When the answer is NO, proceed to the next section*

FAM21. What is your religion?

1. Catholic
2. Traditional Protestant or non-evangelical Protestant (Christian, Calvinist, Lutheran, Methodist, Anglican, Moravian Church, Episcopalian, etc.)
3. Non-Christian Eastern religions (Islam; Buddhist, Hindu; Taoist, Confucianism; Baha'i, etc.)
4. Evangelical and Pentecostal (Pentecostal, Light of the World, Four Square Church, Baptist, Adventist, etc.)
5. Church of Jesus Christ of Latter-Day Saints (Mormons) and traditional religions (Candomblé, Voodoo, Rastafari, Mayan religions, María Lonza, Inti, Kardecista, etc.)
6. Jewish (Orthodox, Conservative or Reformed)
7. Jehovah's Witnesses
8. Other, which?

Studies and Training

EST1. What is the highest level of education you have completed?

1. Bachelor's degree
2. Specialization
3. Master's degree
4. PhD
5. Postdoctorate

EST2. Did you complete any of your studies abroad?

1. Yes
2. No. *If the answer is NO, proceed to question EST4*

EST3. In which country?
EST4. Did you receive your education in a public or a private school?

	Public	*Private*	*Both*	*NS/NR*
Elementary School	[1]	[2]	[3]	[0]
Junior High	[1]	[2]	[3]	[0]
High school	[1]	[2]	[3]	[0]
University	[1]	[2]	[3]	[0]
Master's degree	[1]	[2]	[3]	[0]
Doctorate	[1]	[2]	[3]	[0]
Postdoctoral	[1]	[2]	[3]	[0]

EST5. In what year did you graduate as a lawyer?
EST6. At which university did you complete your undergraduate studies? *If you do not have a master's or PhD, proceed to question EST9*
EST7. At which university did you complete your master's studies? *If you do not have a PhD, go to question EST9*
EST8. At which university did you complete your PhD?
EST9. Which educational model would you say best describes your undergraduate studies?

1. Educational model through master lectures and memorization of legal texts. *If you do not have a doctorate, proceed to question EST11*
2. Educational model that privileges learning through case studies and horizontal discussion between students and professor. *If you do not have a doctorate, proceed to question EST11*

EST10. And for your postgraduate studies?

1. Educational model through master lectures and memorization of legal texts.

2. Educational model that privileges learning through case studies and horizontal discussion between students and the professor.

EST11. To graduate, did you write a thesis?

1. Yes
2. No

EST12. Do you speak any other language besides Spanish?

1. Yes
2. No

EST13. Which one?

1. English
2. French
3. Italian
4. Portuguese
5. Other, which?

EST14. Do you speak any indigenous language?

1. Yes
2. No

EST15. Do you have any publications?

1. Yes
2. No. *When the answer is NO, proceed to the next section*

EST16. What type of publications do you have?

1. Books
2. Articles in academic journals
3. Articles in the official media of the judiciary
4. Columns in the media

Career and Judicial Trajectory

CJ1. Let's talk about your career and trajectory as a judge. Could you tell me what was the first position you held within the judiciary?

1. Judicial officer
2. Bailiffs

3. Projecting lawyer
4. Secretary
5. Judge
6. Magistrate
7. Other, which?

CJ2. How did you get your first job in the judiciary?
CJ3. What year did you join the judiciary?
CJ4. Why did you decide to be part of the judiciary?
CJ5. Which of the following reasons was most important for you to decide to be part of the federal judiciary?

1. The tradition in your family
2. The prestige of the institution
3. The judicial career
4. The salary and labor benefits
5. Contributing to the improvement of the rule of law
6. Contributing to reducing the prevailing injustices in access to justice

CJ6. What is the preceding position you held before getting a position in the judiciary?

1. Bailiffs
2. Projecting lawyer
3. Secretary
4. Judge in the state judiciary
5. Litigant
6. Notary
7. University professor
8. District judge.

CJ7. In what subject or subjects have you worked?

1. Administrative
2. Criminal
3. Civil
4. Commercial
5. Labor
6. Family
7. Electoral
8. Mixed

9. All
10. Other, which?

CJ8. Have you collaborated or do you collaborate with universities as professor?

1. Yes.
2. No.

CJ9. Which one(s)?
CJ10. Have you worked in other institutions, companies, or organizations?

1. Yes
2. No

CJ11. Where?
CJ12. Are you satisfied with your career as a judge or would you prefer to practice another profession?

1. I would like to practice another profession
2. I am satisfied

Speaking of security issues, please tell me how much you agree or disagree with the following statements:

	[1]Strongly disagree	*[2]Disagree*	*[3]Agree*	*[4]Strongly agree*
CJ13. Practicing our profession has become unsafe in recent years				
CJ14. Colleagues close to me fear for their personal safety				
CJ15. Colleagues close to me use escorts or armored cars				
CJ16. Due to my activity as a judge, I have sometimes feared for my personal safety				

CJ16b. How many years would you like to remain in the judiciary? If the answer is until retirement, ask in how many years they retire
CJ17. Immediately after leaving this position, what position would you like to hold?

CJ18. What is the highest position you aspire to reach in your judicial trajectory?

1. Circuit Magistrate
2. Counselor in the Federal Judiciary Council
3. Magistrate of the Electoral Tribunal of the Judicial Power of the Federation.
4. Minister of the Supreme Court of Justice
5. Judge at the Inter-American Court of Human Rights
6. Judge at the International Criminal Court
7. Judge at some other international court
8. Other.

On a scale of 1–10, where 1 means "nothing" and 10 means "a lot," I would like to know to what extent you agree with the following statements. Considering your experience in the judicial career and what you have seen, to what extent do you believe that

	Scale	*NS/NR*
CJ19. Judges with more experience and training have more chances of keeping their position		
CJ20. Judges with more experience and training have more chances of being nominated for a higher position		
CJ21. Judges with good political contacts have more chances of keeping their position		
CJ22. Judges with good political contacts have more chances of being nominated for a higher position		
CJ23. Only the most competitive profiles enter a judicial career		
CJ24. The opposition contest is decisive to become a district judge or circuit magistrate		

CJ25. Throughout your judicial career, have you been subject to administrative sanctions?

1. Yes
2. No

CJ26. Throughout your judicial career, have you been subject to criminal sanctions?

1. Yes
2. No

CJ27. Do you participate or have you participated in any association of judges or lawyers?

1. Yes.
2. No.

CJ28. Which one?

1. National Association of Circuit Magistrates and District Judges of the PJF
2. Mexican Association of Female Judges
3. Mexican Association of Judges
4. National College of Circuit Magistrates and District Judges of the PJF
5. Other

When talking about association with other judges, please tell me how much you agree with the following statements:

	[1]Strongly disagree	*[2]Disagree*	*[3]Somewhat agree*	*[4]Strongly agree*
CJ29. Being associated favors the defense of the guild's interests against external pressures				
CJ30. Being associated favors the advancement of the guild's interests within the judiciary				
CJ31. It is not relevant to be associated with other judges				

Now, let's talk about the workload in the judiciary. I would like to know how much you agree or disagree with the following statements:

	[1]Strongly disagree	*[2]Disagree*	*[3]Somewhat agree*	*[4]Strongly agree*
CJ32. The workload is excessive				
CJ33. Regularly, the time to know and make an informed decision on a case is not enough				

(continued)

(continued)

	[1]Strongly disagree	*[2]Disagree*	*[3]Somewhat agree*	*[4]Strongly agree*
CJ34. I usually continue with my work at home				
CJ35. It is necessary to create more positions in the circuit where I am assigned				

CJ36. Please indicate what is the ideal profile to be a minister of the Supreme Court:

1. Judge with an exclusive judicial career
2. Judge with a judicial career and litigation experience
3. Judge with a judicial career and academic experience
4. Judge with litigation or academic experience
5. Lawyer with experience

Of the current Supreme Court justices, please tell me with whom you feel most affinity:

	First place	*Second place*	*Third place*
CJ37. Margarita Luna Ramos			
CJ38. Arturo Zaldivar Lelo de Larrea			
CJ39. Norma Lucía Piña Hernández			
CJ40. Eduardo Medina Mora			
CJ41. José Ramón Cossio Díaz			
CJ42. José Fernando Franco González Salas			
CJ43. Alfredo Gutiérrez Ortiz Mena			
CJ44. Jorge Mario Pardo Rebolledo			
CJ45. Luis María Aguilar Morales			
CJ46. Alberto Pérez Dayán			
CJ47. Javier Laynez Potysek			

Ideas About Judicial Roles

In this section we are going to talk about the different ideas that judges have about law, politics, and society. I would like to know how much you agree with the following statements. For this, use the following scale from 1 to 10, where 1 means "strongly disagree" and 10 "strongly agree."

	Scale	*NS/NR*
IDE1. In fact, judges are political actors, that is, they are indirectly policy makers		
IDE2. Judges are apolitical actors		
IDE3. Judges should be apolitical, but some are not		
IDE4. Judges create and develop norms		
IDE5. In current democracies, judges have a legislative role		
IDE6. The judge is not limited to applying pre-existing norms: on occasions, the judge has a 'creative' power to establish the applicable norm		
IDE7. Judges should not create law, but only apply the existing norms		
IDE8. The role of judges is to contribute to the formation of a community of equals		
IDE9. The correction of structural inequalities in a society is not the task of the judiciary, but of the executive and legislative power		
IDE10. The judiciary should seek to eradicate the inequalities that exist in society through the constitutional or conventional review of laws		
IDE11. All constitutional norms are fair		

IDE12. Often we talk about the importance of having good judges. In your opinion, what characteristic should a good judge have?

1. Judicial career
2. Judicial career and academic experience
3. Judicial career and litigation experience
4. A broad and substantive idea of justice
5. A vision that favors the vulnerable sectors of society

IDE13. And secondly?

1. Judicial career
2. Judicial career and academic experience
3. Judicial career and litigation experience
4. A broad and substantive idea of justice
5. A vision that favors the vulnerable sectors of society

IDE14. And thirdly?

1. Judicial career
2. Judicial career and academic experience
3. Judicial career and litigation experience
4. A broad and substantive idea of justice
5. A vision that favors the vulnerable sectors of society

IDE15. When discussing constitutionally valid norms and fair norms, in your role as a judge you believe that one should:

1. Decide based on just moral principles
2. Obey only the law, that is, decide based only on constitutionally valid norms, even if they are unfair
3. Weigh up constitutionally valid norms and moral principles in difficult cases

I am going to name a series of sources of law that contribute to the rulings written by judges. I would like to know how much weight each of these factors normally has when you draft a decision. For this, we will use a scale between 1 and 10, where 1 means "not important at all" and 10 means "extremely important." For example, how important are the following for the drafting of a judgment?

	Scale	*NS/NR*
IDE16. The text of the national positive law		
IDE17. The text of the positive law and evaluative criteria		
IDE18. Conventional norms		
IDE19. Your contact with the parties during the process		
IDE20. The needs of society in each particular situation		
IDE21. The values of the community in relation to the case		

And using the same scale, how much importance do you give to the following factors when you draft a judgment?

	Scale	NS/NR
IDE22. The criteria of the Supreme Court on the matter		
IDE23. The criteria of international courts		
IDE24. The opinions of a respected member of the legal community		
IDE25. The opinions of the press on the matter		
IDE26. The opinions of the law makers on the matter		
IDE27. The opinions of the executive on the matter		
IDE28. The opinions of society on the matter		

I am going to read several phrases about legal positions in relation to the different legal theories. Please tell me to what extent you agree or disagree with them. For this, we will use a scale between 1 and 10, where 1 means "strongly disagree" and 10 "strongly agree."

	Scale	NS/NR
IDE29. Most of the judges with whom you interact believe that law is constituted only by norms of positive law		
IDE30. Most of the judges with whom you interact believe that law is constituted both by norms of positive law and by principles		
IDE31. Constitutional norms are always subject to weighing and not to direct application. They can be weighed with moral principles reasoned by judges.		
IDE32. Judges act illegitimately when they creatively interpret a norm and introduce a new rule		
IDE33. Constitutional norms are largely principles that are respected to a greater or lesser extent because they are susceptible to weighing when they come into conflict with each other		
IDE434. Judges should not limit themselves to interpreting the norms of positive law, but they are also enabled to create norms themselves, even if only through the weighing of principles		
IDE35. Judges can consider resorting to interpretation and weighing when there is no rule that applies to the case to be decided, that is, when there is a normative gap		
IDE36. Law contains an authoritative dimension, but also a value-based, axiological dimension		

(continued)

(continued)

	Scale	NS/NR
IDE37. Judges when making a ruling should only consider the written rule, regardless of whether they are fair or unfair		

Opinions on Indigenous Rights

IND1. Changing the subject, now we will talk a little about the relationship between justice and indigenous rights. Have you made any rulings involving the rights of indigenous communities?

1. Yes
2. No.

Considering what would be done in the judiciary to resolve cases where indigenous rights are claimed and from the rulings that you know or have heard of:

	[1]Not frequent	*[2]Rarely*	*[3]Somewhat frequent*	*[4]Very frequent*
IND2. How often do judges use the "SCJN Protocol of Action in Cases Involving Indigenous Rights"?				
IND3. How often do judges request anthropological expert reports to better understand the claimed rights and guide the direction of their ruling?				
IND4. In case an expert report is requested, how often are the arguments from it used to guide the direction of the ruling?				

When deciding cases involving indigenous rights, three models of judicial decisions can be identified. Considering what would be done in the judiciary to resolve cases where these types of rights are claimed, please tell me how widespread you believe is the prevalence of the model in which:

	[1]Not at all widespread	*[2]Slightly widespread*	*[3]Somewhat widespread*	*[4]Very widespread*
IND5. Judges decide based solely on ordinary positive legislation				
IND6. Judges decide based on ordinary legislation and international human rights law, in particular ILO Convention 169 and the United Nations Declaration on Indigenous Peoples				
IND7. Judges decide based on a model that considers the relationship between the ordinary legal system and the normative systems of indigenous peoples				

Now, please tell me how much you agree or disagree with the following statements. For this, we will use a scale between 1 and 10, where 1 means "strongly disagree" and 10 "strongly agree."

	Scale	*NS/NR*
IND8. Of the rulings you are familiar with on indigenous rights, do most of them clearly demonstrate a vision of interlegality and legal pluralism? That is, they take into account the traditions and cultural specificities of indigenous peoples while respecting the precepts of the Constitution and recognizing the existence of their own normative systems (Article 2 CPEUM)		
IND9. Legal pluralism is the prevailing legal culture model in the decisions of judges in Mexico		
IND10. Most judges recognize and guarantee the validity of norms from various legal systems, including those of indigenous peoples		
IND11. The use of international instruments such as ILO Convention 169 or the United Nations Declaration on Indigenous Peoples is widely disseminated in the judiciary when rulings are made on indigenous law		

(continued)

(continued)

	Scale	*NS/NR*
IND12. To respect the cultures of indigenous peoples in certain cases, a balance must be struck that neutralizes the potential of human rights, such as due process, to be in accordance with the normative systems of indigenous peoples		
IND13. To respect the cultures of indigenous peoples and communities in certain cases, rights emanating from ordinary legislation must be neutralized		
IND14. The evidence shows that in all trials where the party is indigenous, there is always an interpreter		
IND15. Indigenous defendants always have a defender who knows their language and culture		

	[1]Never	*[2]Sometimes*	*[3]Almost always*	*[4]Always*
IND16. Considering what normally happens in the judiciary, would you say that judges carry out a substitution of the complaint when necessary and the promoting party is indigenous?				
IND17. Considering what normally happens in the judiciary, would you say that judges request an interpreter to be assigned when the promoting party is indigenous?				
IDE65. Considering what normally happens in the judiciary, the crimes committed by indigenous people are related to their ignorance of the law				

IDE66. Now we are going to talk about your opinion on other rights and freedoms. I am going to read a series of questions. For this, we will use a scale between 1 and 10, where 1 means "strongly disapprove" and 10 "strongly approve." In your personal opinion:

	Scale	NS/NR
IDE38. How strongly do you approve or disapprove of same-sex marriage?		
IDE39. How strongly do you approve or disapprove of the right to abortion?		
IDE40. How strongly do you approve or disapprove of the legalization of marijuana?		
IDE41. How strongly do you approve or disapprove of the decriminalization of drugs in general?		

IDE42. To finish this section, when talking about political trends, it is said that a person is left wing or right wing. On a scale from 1 to 10, where one is left and 10 is right, where would you place yourself politically?

1 Left	2	3	4	5	6	7	8	9	10 Right	NR

Independence

In this section we are going to talk about your opinions regarding the independence of the federal judiciary.

IND1. Taking into account your experience or what you have heard, would you say that political influences on the judiciary are:

1. Not at all widespread
2. Slightly widespread
3. Somewhat widespread
4. Very widespread

IND2. During the last year, were you ever contacted by a superior who tried to influence your decision in a case?

1. Yes
2. No

IND3. Have you heard of any colleague being contacted by a superior to influence a decision in the last 12 months?

1. Yes

2. No

IND4. During the last year, have you ever faced instances of the state obstructing your work to better understand the case and thus guide the direction of your ruling?

1. Yes
2. No

IND4b. During the last year, have you ever faced de facto powers obstructing your work to better understand the case and thus guide the direction of your ruling?

1. Yes
2. No

IND5. During the last year, have you heard of any colleague being contacted by a politician or official to guide a decision?

1. Yes
2. No

IND6. During the last year, have you ever experienced a bribery attempt?

1. Yes
2. No

IND7. Have you heard of any judge who has received a bribe in the last year?

1. Yes
2. No

IND8. In your experience as a judge, would you say that the rulings of the judiciary are obeyed when the interests of the other branches of the state are involved?

1. Never
2. On some occasions
3. Almost always
4. Always

Sociodemographic Variables

SOC1. What is your gender?

1. Male
2. Female
3. Other

SOC2. What is your age in completed years?
SOC3. For statistical purposes, I would ask you to indicate if you consider yourself a person from any of the following ethnic groups:

1. White
2. *Mestizo*
3. Indigenous
4. Afro-descendant
5. Other
6. NS/NR

SOC4. What language did you speak at home when you were a child?

1. Spanish
2. Indigenous language
3. Foreign language

Note

1. This questionnaire is inspired by and takes up many of the questions that appear in the Parliamentary Elites Questionnaire of the University of Salamanca and the Judges Questionnaire of the University of Pittsburgh and USAID. Likewise, several of the questions within the "Ideas about judicial roles" section explore concepts articulated by legal philosophers such as Manuel Atienza, Luigi Ferrajoli, and others in connection with the subject of positivist and post-positivist constitutionalism. Additionally, I took into consideration the "Protocol of action for those involved in dispensing justice in cases pertaining to the rights of individuals, communities, and indigenous peoples" issued by the Supreme Court of Justice of the Nation for the section "Opinions on indigenous rights". I am deeply grateful for the invaluable input and insights provided by colleagues at ITESO, as well as friends who are judges.

Bibliography

Aguiar-Aguilar, A. (2019). *Government and Judicial Politics in Mexico*. Fontamara, IIJ-UNAM, TEPJF.

Aguiar-Aguilar, A. (2022). Understanding the Judiciary from the Inside. The Legal Culture of Judges in Mexico. *Justice System Journal, 43*(4), 576–592. https://doi.org/10.1080/0098261X.2022.2123288

Aguiar-Aguilar, A., & Torres, I. (2022). Explaining the Sources of Judges' Legal Conceptions in the Mexican Judiciary. *Latin American Law Review, 9*, 117–137.

Ai Camp, R. (2002). *Mexico's Mandarins: Crafting a Power Elite for the Twenty-First Century*. University of California Press.

Alcántara, M. (2014). Some General and Introductory Considerations to the Study of Political Elites in Latin America. *Iberoamericana, 14*(54), 155–159.

Alexy, R. (1994). *The Concept and Validity of Law*. Gedisa.

Almond, G. A. (1988). Separate Tables: Schools and Sects in Political Science. *PS: Political Science and Politics, 21* (4), 828–842. https://doi.org/10.2307/420022

Ansolabehere, K. (2007). *Politics from Justice: Supreme Courts, Government and Democracy in Argentina and Mexico*. Distribuciones Fontamara.

Ansolabehere, K. (2008). Legalists, Moderate Legalists and Moderate Guarantors: Legal Ideology of Teachers, Judges, Lawyers, Public Prosecutors and Deputies. *Mexican Journal of Sociology, 70*(2), 331–349.

Ansolabehere, K. (2010). More Power, More Rights? The Supreme Court and Society in Mexico. In J. Couso, A. Huneeus, & R. Sieder (Eds.), *Cultures*

A. A. Aguiar Aguilar, *Legal Culture, Sociopolitical Origins and Professional Careers of Judges in Mexico*,
https://doi.org/10.1007/978-3-031-52909-2

of Legality: Judicialization and Political Activism in Latin America (pp. 78–111). Cambridge University Press.

Ansolabehere, K., Botero, S., & González-Ocantos, E. (2023). Conceptualizing and Measuring Legal Culture. Evidence from a Survey of Mexican Federal Judges. *Politics and Government*. CIDE.

Arellano, A. (2012). Trajectories, Networks and Recruitment Mechanisms in the Supreme Court of Jalisco. *Sociological Studies of the College of Mexico, 30*(88), 87–118.

Atienza, M. (2006). *Law as Argumentation*. Ariel Law.

Atienza, M. (2009). Impartiality and the Ibero-American Model Code of Judicial Ethics. *Studies of Judicial Law, 151*, 167–186.

Atienza, M. (2011a). Two Versions of Constitutionalism. *Doxa: Notebooks of Philosophy of Law*, (34), 73–88.

Atienza, M. (2011b, April). How to Unmask a Formalist. *Isonomy, 34*.

Atienza, M., & Ruíz, J. (2007, October). Let's Leave Behind Legal Positivism. *Isonomy, 27*, 7–28.

Atienza, M., & Ruíz, J. (2009). *For a Postpositivist Theory of Law*. TEMIS.

Atkinson, R., & Flint, J. (2001). Accessing Hidden and Hard-to-Reach Populations: Snowball Research Strategies. *Social Research Update, 33*, 1–4.

Baldassarri, D., & Abascal, M. (2017). Field Experiments across the Social Sciences. *The Annual Review of Sociology, 43*(1), 41–73.

Bárcena, E. (2018). Judicial Reproduction and Legal Culture. The System of Appointment of Personnel in the Mexican Supreme Court. *Oñati Socio-legal Series, 8*(5), 739–759.

Barragán, M. (2015). The Study of Parliamentary Elites in Latin America. Past, Present and Future. *Andean Journal of Political Studies, 5*(2), 4–30.

Barragán, M., Rivas, C., & Bohigues García, A. (2020). Latin American Parliamentary Elites: How has the Profile of Representation Evolved? *Spanish Journal of Sociology, 29*(3), 613–633.

Barrera, L. (2012). *The Supreme Court on stage: An Ethnography of the Judicial World*. Siglo XXI Publishers.

Basabe-Serrano, S. (2014). Determinants of Judicial Dissent in Contexts of Extreme Institutional Instability: The Case of Ecuador's Constitutional Court. *Journal of Politics in Latin America, 6*(1), 83–107.

Beer, C. (2006). Judicial Performance and the Rule of Law in the Mexican States. *Latin American Politics and Society, 48*(3), 33–61.

Best, H., & Cotta, M. (2000). Elite Transformation and Modes of Representation since the Mid-Nineteenth Century: Some Theoretical Considerations. In H. Best & M. Cotta (Eds.), *Parliamentary Representatives in Europe 1848–2000. Legislative recruitments and Careers in Eleven European Countries* (pp. 1–28). Oxford University Press.

Blackstone, W. (1983). *Commentaries on the Laws of England* (Vol. 1). Clarendon Press.

Boyd, C., Epstein, L., & Martin, A. (2010). Untangling the Causal Effects of Sex on Judging. *American Journal of Political Science, 54*(2), 389–411.

Brigido, A., & Lista, C. (2009). Legal Education in the University in the Face of Reforms in the Judiciary. *Notebooks of Education, 7*, 325–340.

Brinks, D. (2008). *The Judicial Response to Police Killings in Latin America: Inequality and the Rule of Law*. Cambridge University Press.

Borrego, F. (2017). Study on Family and Client Networks in the Federal Judiciary Council. *Mexican Journal of Justice, 29–30*, 159–191.

Caballero, J. (2006). The Jurisdictional Profile of Federal Judges. *Journal of the Federal Judiciary Institute, 22*, 281–312.

Carbonell, M. (2000). Judicial Power and Transition to Democracy: The 1999 Reform. *Mexican Bulletin of Comparative Law, 97*, 329–350.

Carbonell, M. (2007). *Theory of Neoconstitutionalism. Selected Essays*. Trotta, IJJ-UNAM.

Carpizo, J. (2001). Twenty-two Years of Mexican Presidentialism: 1978–2000. A Recapitulation. *Mexican Bulletin of Comparative Law, 24*(100), 71–99.

Castagnola, A. (2018). *Manipulating Courts in New Democracies: Forcing Judges off the Bench in Argentina*. Routledge.

Castagnola, A., & López, S. (2016). *The Role of the Supreme Court in Mexico's Democratic Consolidation*. Tirant lo Blanch, IIJ UNAM.

Castillejos-Aragón, M. (2013). The Transformation of the Mexican Supreme Court into an Arena for Political Contestation. In G. Silverstein, D. Kapiszewski & R. Kagan (Eds.), *Consequential Courts. Judicial Roles in Global Perspective* (pp. 138–160). Cambridge University Press.

Castillo, P. (2016). *EU Treaties and the Judicial Politics of National Courts. A Law and Politics Approach*. Routledge.

Chávez, R. (2004). *The Rule of Law in Nascent Democracies: Judicial Politics in Argentina*. Stanford University Press.

Coke, Sir Edward. (1986). *Institutes of the Laws of England I*. J.H. Thomas Ed.

Concha Cantú Hugo and José Antonio Caballero Juárez. (2001). *Diagnosis on the Administration of Justice in the Federal Entities. An Institutional Study on Local Justice in Mexico*. IIJ-UNAM.

Cortez, J. (2014). Comparative Qualitative Analysis: The Decisions of the Supreme Court Against the Executive in Mexico. *Mexican Journal of Sociology, 76*(3), 413–439.

Cortez, J. (2019). Study and Account Secretaries in the Supreme Court of Mexico: An Essential but Forgotten Actor. *Politics and Government, 26*(2), 219–236.

Cortez, J. (2020). *Ideas, Innovation and Organizational Change in the Supreme Court of Justice of the Nation*. IIJ-UNAM.

Cortés, N., Rodríguez, O., & Shirk, D. (2016). *Justicebarometer 2016. Perspectives of the Criminal Justice System in Mexico: What Do its Operators Think?* Justice in Mexico.

Cossío, J. R. (1996). *Notebooks for Judicial Reform: Federal Jurisdiction and Judicial Career in Mexico.* Mexico: IIJ-UNAM.

Cotterrell, R. (1997). The Concept of Legal Culture. In D. Nelken (Ed.), *Comparing Legal Cultures* (pp. 13–32). Dartmouth Publishing Company.

Couso, J. (2005). The Judicialization of Chilean Politics: The Rights Revolution That Never Was. In R. Sieder, L. Schjolden, & A. Angell (Eds.), *The Judicialization of Politics in Latin America* (pp. 105–129). Palgrave Macmillan.

Couso, J. (2010). The Transformation of Constitutional Discourse and the Judicialization of Politics in Latin America. In J. Couso, A. Huneeus, & R. Sieder (Eds.), *Cultures of Legality: Judicialization and Political Activism in Latin America* (pp. 141–160). Cambridge University Press.

Couso, J., & Hilbink, L. (2011). From Quietism to Incipient Activism. In G. Helmke & J. Rios-Figueroa (Eds.), *Courts in Latin America* (pp. 99–127). Cambridge University Press.

Couso, J., Huneeus, A., & Sieder, R. (2010). *Cultures of Legality: Judicialization and Political Activism in Latin America.* Cambridge University Press.

Cuéllar, A. (2008). *The Judges of Tradition. A Case Study.* FCPyS-UNAM.

Dahl, R. (1961). *Who Governs? Democracy and Power in an American City.* Yale University Press.

Di Federico, G. (2005). *Recruitment, Professional Evaluation and Career of Judges and Prosecutors in Europe: Austria, France, Germany, Italy, the Netherlands and Spain.* Lo Scarabeo.

Domingo, P. (2000). Judicial Independence: The Politics of the Supreme Court in Mexico. *Journal of Latin American Studies, 32*(3), 705–735.

Donatello, L., & Lorenc, F. (2017). The Rise to the Judicial Elite. A Reconstruction of the Origins and Trajectories of Judges from Biographical Interviews. *Argentine Sociology Journal, 11*(19–20), 6–29.

Dworkin, R. (1986). *Law's Empire.* Harvard University Press.

Epstein, L., & Knight, J. (1998). *The Choices Justices Make.* Congressional Quarterly Press.

Epstein, L., & Knight, J. (2000). Toward a Strategic Revolution in Judicial Politics: A Look Back, A Look Ahead. *Political Research Quarterly, 53*(3), 625–661.

Epstein, L., & Martin, A. (2014). *An Introduction to Empirical Legal Research.* Oxford University Press.

Equis Justice. (2021). *Open Justice: From Opacity to Judicial Openness. Ranking of Judicial Transparency in Mexico 2021.* Equis Justice for Women.

Ferejohn, J. (2002). Judicializing Politics, Politicizing Law. *Law and Contemporary Problems, 65*(3), 41–68.
Ferrajoli, L. (2011). Principalist Constitutionalism and Guarantor Constitutionalism. *Doxa: Philosophy of Law Notebooks,* (34), 15–53.
Ferreyra, G. (2018). Unpacking the Mexican Federal Judiciary: An Inner Look at the Ethos of the Judicial Branch. *Mexican Law Review, 11*(1), 57–83.
Field, A., Miles, J., & Field, Z. (2012). *Discovering Statistics Using R*. Sage Publications Ltd.
Finkel, J. (2008). *Judicial Reform as Political Insurance: Argentina, Peru, and Mexico in the 1990s*. University of Notre Dame Press.
Fix-Fierro, H. (1996). The Defense of Constitutionality in the Judicial Reform of 1994. *Constitutional Notebooks Mexico-Central America, 19*, 41–57.
Fix-Fierro, H. (1999). Judicial Power. In M. del Refugio & S. López-Ayllón (Eds.), *Transitions and Institutional Designs* (pp. 167–221). UNAM.
Fix-Fierro, H. (2020). *The Power of the Judiciary and the Legal Modernization in Contemporary Mexico.* IIJ-UNAM.
Fix-Zamudio, H. (1997). Brief Reflections on the Council of the Judiciary. In National Autonomous University of Mexico, *Mexican Justice Toward the 21st Century* (pp. 139–187). UNAM.
Friedman, L. (1969). Legal Culture and Social Development. *Law & Society Review, 4*(1), 29–44.
Friedman, L. (1975). *The Legal System: A Social Science Perspective*. Russell Sage Foundation.
Friedman, L. (1997). The Concept of Legal Culture. A Reply. In D. Nelken (Ed.), *Comparing Legal Cultures* (pp. 33–40). Dartmouth Publishing Company.
Garapon, A. (1995). French Legal Culture and the Shock of 'Globalization.' *Social & Legal Studies, 4*(4), 493–506.
Garapon, A. (1997). *Judging Well. Essay on the Judicial Ritual*. Odile Jacob.
Garoupa, N., & Ginsburg, T. (2009). Guarding the Guardians: Judicial Councils and Judicial Independence. *The American Journal of Comparative Law, 57*(1), 103–134.
Garoupa, N., & Ginsburg, T. (2011). Hybrid Judicial Career Structures: Reputation versus Legal Tradition. *Journal of Legal Analysis, 3*(2), 411–448.
Garoupa, N., Gili, M., & Gómez-Pomar, F. (2012). Political Influence and Career Judges: An Empirical Analysis of Administrative Review by the Spanish Supreme Court. *Journal of Empirical Legal Studies, 9*(4), 795–826.
George, A., & Bennett, A. (2005). *Case Studies and Theory Development in the Social Sciences*. MIT Press.
Georgakopoulos, N. (2000). Discretion in the Career and Recognition Judiciary. *Chicago Law School Roundtable, 7*(1), 205–225.

Gerring, J., & Cojocaru, L. (2016). Selecting Cases for Intensive Analysis: A Diversity of Goals and Methods. *Sociological Methods & Research, 45*(3), 392–423.

Gibson, J., & Caldeira, G. (1996). The Legal Cultures of Europe. *Law and Society Review, 30*(1), 55–86.

Ginsburg, T. (2003). *Judicial Review in New Democracies. Constitutional Courts in Asian Countries*. Cambridge University Press.

Goertz, G. (2017). *Multimethod Research, Causal Mechanisms, and Case Studies: An Integrated Approach*. Princeton University Press.

González-Ocantos, E. (2016). *Shifting Legal Visions: Judicial Change and Human Rights Trials in Latin America*. Cambridge University Press.

Guarnieri, C. (2003). *Justice and Politics. The Knots of the Second Republic*. Il Mulino.

Guarnieri, C. (2004). Appointment and Career of Judges in Continental Europe: The Rise of Judicial Self-Government. *Legal Studies, 24*(1–2), 169–187.

Guarnieri, C. (2008). Magistrates in Europe: Independence, Professionalism, Responsibility: The Italian Case. *Studi Urbinati, A - Juridical, Political and Economic Sciences, 59*(2), 255–264.

Guarnieri, C. (2011). *Berlusconi on Trial: Some Lessons for Judicial Accountability*. The Foundation for Law, Justice and Society.

Guarnieri, C., & Pederzoli, P. (2002). *The Judiciary in Contemporary Democracies*. Editori Laterza.

Hammergren, L. (1998). *The Politics of Justice and Justice Reform in Latin America: The Peruvian Case in Comparative Perspective*. Westview.

Hart, H. (1958). Positivism and the Separation of Law and Morals. *Harvard Law Review, 71*(4), 593–629.

Helmke, G. (2004). *Courts Under Constraints: Judges, Generals, and Presidents in Argentina*. Cambridge University Press.

Hilbink, L. (2007). *Judges Beyond Politics in Democracy and Dictatorship: Lessons from Chile*. Cambridge University Press.

Inclán, S. (2009). Judicial Reform in Mexico: Political Insurance or the Search for Political Legitimacy? *Political Research Quarterly, 62*(4), 753–766.

Ingram, M. (2012). Crafting Courts in New Democracies. Ideology and Judicial Council Reform in Three Mexican States. *Comparative Politics, 44*(4), 439–458.

Ingram, M. (2016a). *Crafting Courts in New Democracies. The Politics of Subnational Judicial Reform in Brazil and Mexico*. Cambridge University Press.

Ingram, M. (2016b). Networked Justice: Judges, the Diffusion of Ideas, and Legal Reform Movements in Mexico. *Journal of Latin American Studies, 48*(4), 739–768.

Ingram, M. (2019). Interviews. Judicial Politics in the Voice of the Experts. In A. Aguiar-Aguilar (Ed.), *Government and Judicial Politics in Mexico* (pp. 172–193). Fontamara, IIJ-UNAM, TEPJF.

Ingram, M., & Kapiszewski, D. (2019). *Beyond High Courts: The Justice Complex in Latin America*. University of Notre Dame Press.

Johnson, R., Onwuegbuzie, A., & Turner, L. (2007). Toward a Definition of Mixed Methods Research. *Journal of Mixed Methods Research, 1*(2), 112–133.

Kapiszewski, D. (2012). *High Courts and Economic Governance in Argentina and Brazil*. Cambridge University Press.

Kapiszewski, D., & Taylor, M. (2008). Doing Courts Justice? Studying Judicial Politics in Latin America. *Perspectives on Politics, 6*(4), 741–767.

Kapiszewski, D., MacLean, L., & Read, B. (2015). *Field Research in Political Science*. Cambridge University Press.

Lyberg, L., Stange, M., Harkness, J., Mohler, P., Pennell, B., & Japec, L. (2014). A Review of Quality Issues Associated with Studying Hard-to-Survey Populations. In R. Tourangeau, B. Edwards, T. Johnson, K. Wolter, & N. Bates (Eds.), *Hard-to-Survey Populations* (pp. 82–108). Cambridge University Press.

Latinobarómetro. (2021). *2021 Report. Goodbye to Macondo*. Latinobarómetro Corporation.

Latour, B. (2010). *The Making of Law: An Ethnography of the Conseil d'Etat*. Polity Press.

La Porta, R., López-de-Silanes, F., Pop-Eleches, C., & Shleifer, A. (2001). Judicial Checks and Balances. *Journal of Political Economy, 112*(2), 445–470.

Lista, C., & Brigido, A. (2002). *The Teaching of Law and the Formation of Legal Consciousness*. Sima Publisher.

Lindón, A. (1999). Autobiographical Narratives, Memory and Myths: An Approach to Social Action. *Economy, Society and Territory, 2*(6), 295–310.

López-Ayllón, S., & Valladares, F. (2009). The Actions of Unconstitutionality in the Mexican Constitution: Empirical Balance of Twelve Years of Exercise. *Constitutional Issues, 21*, 175–211.

Magaloni, A. (2006). Bottlenecks and Windows of Opportunity for Reform and Elite Legal Education in Mexico. In H. Fix-Fierro (Ed.), *From the Government of Lawyers to the Empire of Laws. Socio-legal Studies on Education and Legal Profession in Contemporary Mexico* (pp. 61–91). IIJ-UNAM.

Magaloni, A. (2008). Why has the Supreme Court Not Been an Instrument for the Defense of Fundamental Rights? In A. Zaldívar & E. Ferrer (Eds.), *The Science of Constitutional Procedural Law. Studies in Homage to Héctor Fix-Zamudio on his Fifty Years as a Researcher of Law. II Constitutional Courts and Democracy* (pp. 271–289). IJJ-UNAM.

Magaloni, B. (2003). Authoritarianism, Democracy and the Supreme Court: Horizontal Exchange and the Rule of Law in Mexico. In S. Mainwaring &

C. Welna (Eds.), *Democratic Accountability in Latin America* (pp. 266–306). Oxford University Press.

Michel, E. (2014, October 31). Pardo Rebolledo, Dreamed of Being a Minister Since He was a Child. *El Universal.*

Mijangos, P. (2019). *Minimal History of the Supreme Court of Justice of Mexico.* El Colegio de México.

Montaño, M. (2017). Introduction. In F. Patrón & M. Montaño (Eds.), *Local Parliamentary Elites in Mexico: Attitudes and Performance* (pp. 13–24). Tirant Lo Blanch.

Murphy, W., & Pritchett, H. (1961). *Courts, Judges and Politics.* Random House.

Nelken, D. (1995). Disclosing/Invoking Legal Culture: An Introduction. *Social & Legal Studies, 4*(4), 435–452.

Nelken, D. (1997). *Comparing Legal Cultures.* Dartmouth Publishing Company.

Nelken, D. (2004). Using the Concept of Legal Culture. *Australian Journal of Legal Philosophy, 29*, 2–26.

Nunes, R. (2010). Ideational Origins of Progressive Judicial Activism: The Colombian Constitutional Court and the Right to Health. *Latin American Politics and Society, 52*(3), 67–97.

Owens, R., Tahk, A., Wohlfarth, P., & Bryan, A. (2015). Nominating Commissions, Judicial Retention, and Forward-Looking Behavior on State Supreme Courts: An Empirical Examination of Selection and Retention Methods. *State Politics & Policy Quarterly, 15*(2), 211–238.

Pásara, L. (2010). *Three Keys to Justice in Peru.* Fondo Editorial de la PUCP.

Pérez-Liñán, A., Ames, B., & Seligson, M. (2006). Strategy, Careers, and Judicial Decisions: Lessons from the Bolivian Courts. *The Journal of Politics, 68*(2), 284–295.

Pérez-Perdomo, R., & Friedman, L. (2003). Latin Legal Cultures in the Age of Globalization. In R. Pérez-Perdomo & L. Friedman (Eds.), *Legal Culture in the Age of Globalization. Latin America and Latin Europe* (pp. 1–19). Stanford University Press.

Phillips, T. (2009). The Merits of Merit Selection. *Harvard Journal of Law & Public Policy, 32*(1), 67–96.

Piana, D. (2010). *Judicial Accountabilities in New Europe. From Rule of Law to Quality of Justice.* Routledge.

Pozas-Loyo, A., & Ríos-Figueroa, J. (2010). Enacting Constitutionalism. The Origins of Independent Judicial Institutions in Latin America. *Comparative Politics, 42*(3), 293–311.

Pozas-Loyo, A., & Ríos-Figueroa, J. (2018). Anatomy of an Informal Institution: The 'Gentlemen's Pact' and Judicial Selection in Mexico, 1917–1994. *International Political Science Review, 39*(5), 647–661.

Pozas-Loyo, A., & Ríos-Figueroa, J. (2021). "Enderezar el Derecho: por la regulación de la educación y profesión jurídicas y contra la discriminación por género." Mexicanos Contra la Corrupción. https://contralacorrupcion.mx/wp-content/uploads/2021/03/enderezar-el-derecho-andrea-pozas-julio-rios.pdf

Rachlinski, J., Guthrie, C., & Wistrich, A. (2006). Inside the Bankruptcy Judge's Mind. *Boston University Law Review, 86*(5), 1227–1265.

Ríos, V. (2020, July 6). No, You are Not Middle Class. *The New York Times*.

Ríos-Figueroa, J. (2007). Fragmentation of Power and the Emergence of an Effective Judiciary in Mexico, 1994–2002. *Latin American Politics and Society, 49*(1), 31–57.

Ríos-Figueroa, J. (2011). Institutions for Constitutional Justice in Latin America. In G. Helmke & J. Rios-Figueroa (Eds.), *Courts in Latin America* (pp. 27–54). Cambridge University Press.

Ríos-Figueroa, J. (2018, August 27). The Meritocratic Deficit. Nepotism and Family Networks in the Federal Judicial Power. *Nexos*.

Robinson, R., & Swedlow, B. (2018). Beyond Liberal and Conservative: Advancing the Study of Judicial Behavior with a Cultural Theory of Political Values. *Journal of Law and Courts, 6*(2), 263–302.

Saavedra Herrera, Camilo. (2020). The Keys to the Supreme Court: "Political Fragmentation and Constitutional Litigation in Mexico. *Mexican Journal of Sociology, 82*(2).

Saba, R. (2016). *Beyond Formal Equality Before the Law. What Does the State Owe to Disadvantaged Groups?* Siglo XXI Editores.

Sadek, M. (2006). *Magistrates: An Image in Motion*. Editora FGV.

Sadek, M. (2010). The Judiciary Crisis seen by Judges: Results of a Quantitative Research. In M. Sadek (Ed.), *An Introduction to the Study of Justice* (pp. 17–31). Centro Edelstein of Social Research.

Sánchez, A., Magaloni, B., & Magar, E. (2011). Legalist vs. Interpretativist: The Supreme Court and the Democratic Transition in Mexico. In G. Helmke & J. Ríos-Figueroa (Eds.), *Courts in Latin America* (pp. 187–218). Cambridge University Press.

Sartori, G. (1970). Concept Misformation in Comparative Politics. *The American Political Science Review, 64*(4), 1033–1053.

Sarrabayrouse, M. (2001). Local Legal Cultures: Between Egalitarianism and Hierarchies. *Social Anthropology Notebooks, 13*, 205–228.

Segal, J., & Spaeth, H. (1993). *The Supreme Court and the Attitudinal Model*. Cambridge University Press.

Sieder, R., Schjolden, L., & Angell, A. (Eds.). (2005). *The Judicialization of Politics in Latin America*. Palgrave Macmillan.

Schedler, A. (2006). *Electoral Authoritarianism: The Dynamics of Unfree Competition*. Lynne Rienner Publishers.

Scheppele, K. (2004). Constitutional Ethnography: An Introduction. *Law & Society Review, 38*(3), 389–406.

Shapiro, M. (1963). Political Jurisprudence. *Kentucky Law Journal, 52*(2), 294–345.

Shapiro, M. (1964). *Law and Politics in the Supreme Court*. The Free Press of Glencoe.

Shapiro, M. (1981). *Courts. A Comparative and Political Analysis*. The University of Chicago Press.

Silbey, S. (2010). Legal Culture and Cultures of Legality. In J. Hall, L. Grindstaff, & M. Lo (Eds.), *Handbook of Cultural Sociology* (pp. 470–479). Routledge.

SCJN. (2016). *Profiles of the Ministers of the Supreme Court of Justice of the Nation. 1917–2016*. SCJN.

Smith, T. (2014). Hard-to-Survey Populations in Comparative Perspective. In R. Tourangeau, B. Edwards, T. Johnson, K. Wolter, & N. Bates (Eds.), *Hard-to-Survey Populations* (pp. 21–36). Cambridge University Press.

Spamann, H., & Klöhn, L. (2016). Justice is Less Blind, and Less Legalistic, than We Thought: Evidence from an Experiment with Real Judges. *The Journal of Legal Studies, 45*(2), 255–280.

Staton, J. (2008). Formal Theory in Comparative Judicial Politics. *Law & Courts, 18*(3), 10–15.

Stone Sweet, Alec. (2000). *Governing with Judges: Constitutional Politics in Europe*. Oxford University Press.

Strother, L., & Glennon, C. (2021). An Experimental Investigation of the Effect of Supreme Court Justices' Public Rhetoric on Perceptions of Judicial Legitimacy. *Law & Social Inquiry, 46*(2), 435–454.

Taylor, C. (2009). Merit Selection: Choosing Judges Based on Their Politics under the Veil of a Disarming Name. *Harvard Journal of Law & Public Policy, 32*(1), 97–101.

Tourangeau, R. (2014). Defining hard-to-survey populations. In R. Tourangeau, B. Edwards, T. Johnson, K. Wolter, & N. Bates (Eds.), *Hard-to-Survey Populations* (pp. 3–20). Cambridge University Press.

Trochev, A. (2008). *Judging Russia: The Role of Constitutional Court in Russian Politics*. Cambridge University Press.

Verzelloni, L. (2012). Behind the Judges' desk: An Ethnographic Study on the Italian Courts of Justice. *International Journal for Court Administration, 4*(2), 75–83.

Waldron, J. (2018). *Against the Government of the Judges. Advantages and Disadvantages of Making Decisions by Majority in Congress and in the Courts*. Siglo XXI Editores.

Werneck, L., Rezende, M., Cunha, M., & Baumann, M. (1997). *Body and Soul of the Brazilian Magistracy*. Revan.

Whittington, K. (2007). *Political Foundations of Judicial Supremacy: The Presidency, the Supreme Court, and Constitutional Leadership in U.S. History*. Princeton University Press.

Wickham, H. (2016). *Ggplot2: Elegant Graphics for Data Analysis*. Springer-Verlag.

Zagrebelsky, G. (2003). Ronald Dworkin's Principle Based Constitutionalism. *International Journal of Constitutional Law, 1*(4), 621–650.

Other Sources

ANMJ-PJF. (2022). About JUFED. https://jufed.org/

Hartmann, K., Krois, J., & Waske, B. (2018). *E-Learning Project SOGA: Statistics and Geospatial Data Analysis*. Freie Universitaet Berlin.

INEGI. (2019). National Census of Federal Justice Administration 2019. Mexico.

INEGI. (2020). Population and Housing Census 2020. Mexico.

R Core Team. (2019). R: A Language and Environment for Statistical Computing. R Foundation for Statistical Computing, Vienna, Austria. https://www.R-project.org/

SJCN. Constitutional Controversies and Actions of Unconstitutionality Resolved by the Plenary. https://www.scjn.gob.mx/pleno/seccion-tramite-controversias

SCJN. (2013). "Contradiction of thesis 299/2013." Weekly Judicial of the Federation. https://sjf.scjn.gob.mx/sjfsist/paginas/DetalleGeneralV2.aspx?id=25944&Clase=DetalleTesisEjecutorias

SJCN. "Section of Processing of Constitutional Controversies and of Actions of Unconstitutionality." https://www.scjn.gob.mx/pleno/seccion-tramite-controversias

Valle-Jones, D. (2020). Mxmaps - Create Maps of Mexico. https://www.diegovalle.net/mxmaps/

Index

A. A. Aguiar Aguilar, *Legal Culture, Sociopolitical Origins and Professional Careers of Judges in Mexico*,
https://doi.org/10.1007/978-3-031-52909-2

FSC
www.fsc.org
MIX
Papier | Fördert gute Waldnutzung
FSC® C083411

Kolibri 360 GmbH
Ferdinand-Jühlke-Straße 7
99095 Erfurt, Deutschland
produktsicherheit@kolibri360.de